Essential
Edinburgh

by Sally Roy

Sally Roy is a freelance Scottish travel
writer who has written and contributed
to numerous guides on Scotland and Europe.
She has known and loved Edinburgh all her
life, and has lived there on and off for more
than 20 years. Other books for the AA include
the *AA Road Book of Britain* and
AA Essential Costa Blanca.

Above: *the silhouette of Edinburgh Castle soars
above The Lawnmarket*

AA Publishing

Written by Sally Roy

Published and distributed in the United Kingdom by AA Publishing, a trading name of Automobile Association Developments Limited, whose registered office is Norfolk House, Priestley Road, Basingstoke, Hampshire, RG24 9NY.
Registered number 1878835.

Above: the Edinburgh Festival Hub provides a year-round taste of August's extravaganza

Front cover: Edinburgh Castle; Festival fireworks; Scots piper

Back cover: a tin of Edinburgh rock

A CIP catalogue record for this book is available from the British Library.

ISBN 0 7495 2300 X

The contents of this publication are believed correct at the time of printing. Nevertheless, the publishers cannot be held responsible for any errors or omissions or for changes in the details given in this guide or for the consequences of any reliance on the information it provides. Assessments of attractions, hotels, restaurants and other sights are based upon the author's personal experience and, therefore, necessarily contain elements of subjective opinion which may not reflect the publisher's opinion or dictate a reader's own experience on another occasion.

We have tried to ensure accuracy in this guide, but things do change and we would be grateful if readers would advise us of any inaccuracies they may encounter.

Colour separation: Chroma Graphics (Overseas) Pte Ltd, Singapore
Printed and bound in Italy by Printer Trento S.r.l

Find out more about AA Publishing and the wide range of services the AA provides by visiting our web site at www.theaa.co.uk

Contents

About this Book

Essential *Edinburgh* is divided into five sections to cover the most important aspects of your visit to Edinburgh.

Viewing Edinburgh pages 5–14
An introduction to Edinburgh by the author.
Edinburgh's Features
Essence of Edinburgh
The Shaping of Edinburgh
Peace and Quiet
Edinburgh's Famous

Top Ten pages 15–26
The author's choice of the Top Ten places to see in Edinburgh, each with practical information.

What to See pages 27–90
The four main areas in and around Edinburgh, each with its own brief introduction and an alphabetical listing of the main attractions.
Practical information
Snippets of 'Did you know…' information
4 suggested walks
2 suggested tours
2 features

Where To… pages 91–116
Detailed listings of the best places to eat, stay, shop, take the children and be entertained.

Practical Matters pages 117–24
A highly visual section containing essential travel information.

Maps
All map references are to the individual maps found in the What to See section of this guide.

For example, Edinburgh Castle has the reference ➕ 28C2 – indicating the page on which the map is located and the grid square in which the castle is to be found. A list of the maps that have been used in this travel guide can be found in the index.

Prices
Where appropriate, an indication of the cost of an establishment is given by **£** signs:
£££ denotes higher prices, **££** denotes average prices, while **£** denotes lower charges.

Star Ratings
Most of the places described in this book have been given a separate rating:
❂❂❂ Do not miss
❂❂ Highly recommended
❂ Worth seeing

Viewing Edinburgh

Above: *splendid interior decoration at the head office of the Royal Bank of Scotland*
Right: *viewing 18th-century sartorial elegance at the National Gallery*

Sally Roy's Edinburgh

Enjoying a pause at a pavement café on the Royal Mile

It's always hard to view a much-loved city dispassionately – memories and habits get in the way. Edinburgh for me conjures up visits to the dentist and shopping for school uniform, drives to the city to enjoy the Festival as a student, getting to know it ever better during the 20-odd years I lived there.

I still love Edinburgh; no one could be lukewarm about a city so harmonious and civilised. 'Fur coat and nae knickers' say the city's detractors, but there's little wrong with keeping up appearances and presenting one's best face to the world. And what a face. From the cobblestones of the Royal Mile, lined with a glorious jumble of ancient tenements, to the cool restrained splendour of the New Town terraces, there's always something to delight the eye. The big set pieces – the Castle, Holyrood, medieval and classical Edinburgh – never disappoint, but there's so much else beside. The hidden wynds (narrow lanes) and closes of the Old Town, the quiet streets and tucked-away mews in the New, the smug and comfortable villas in the tree-lined avenues of Morningside are all just as much essential elements in the townscape as is the brooding presence of Arthur's Seat. Even the bleak outer housing estates and the squalor behind the glories are part of the package, ingredients that balance what might otherwise be bland perfection.

Take time to enjoy it all: a marvellous city whose attractions are set against a glorious backdrop, and whose people are amongst the kindest and couthiest you could hope to meet.

When To Go
The vast majority of Edinburgh's tourists come north during the summer, particularly during August, the Festival month. Undoubtedly, the city is then at its liveliest, but it's also crowded, noisy and chaotic. For truly pleasurable sightseeing May, June and September are the ideal months, with a better-than-average chance of good weather. If you don't mind cold, wet and wind, the winter months are the time to experience the city at its most uncrowded and atmospheric.

Contrasting shapes add to the architectural interest of Edinburgh's skyline

Edinburgh's Features

Geography

* Edinburgh lies a little south of the Firth of Forth by Scotland's east coast.
* The city's highest point is Arthur's Seat, 251m, while the seaport of Leith and the waterside areas of Newhaven, Portobello and Cramond lie at sea level.
* The Water of Leith runs northeast, passing through Edinburgh and reaching the Firth of Forth at Leith.

Climate

Edinburgh has a climate which is typical of the northeastern coast; fairly dry and windy, with lowish average temperatures. Although drier than Scotland's west coast, it can rain at any time. Winter will normally bring frosts and snow, even in the city centre, though the snow does not normally lie for long. In summer, the east coast sea-mists, known as 'haar', can affect the city.

The City

Edinburgh is a compact city with its population living within the natural boundary of the Firth of Forth to the north and the southern bypass. Within the city there are 30 designated conservation areas and over 3,000 listed buildings.

Economy

Edinburgh is the second-largest financial and administrative centre in Britain, the majority of employment being provided by service activities; insurance and banking are the prime sectors. Large numbers are employed in healthcare, local government, and, since devolution in 1999, in Scottish national government. Tourism is also of economic importance.

Arthur's Seat rises majestically above Holyrood Park

A Few Figures
Projected population of Edinburgh in 2001: 452,000
Price in £s of a top-rate set of bagpipes: 2, 850
Price in £s of a made-to-measure kilt: 350
Length in miles of the Water of Leith: 22
Average number of January days with snow lying: 5

7

Essence of Edinburgh

Inset: *a display of traditional Scottish dancing in Princes Street Gardens*
Below: *street theatre on the Royal Mile draws crowds in the Festival*

Edinburgh is the capital of Scotland, with everything a capital should have – a sense of history, superb architecture, great museums and a vibrant cultural life. Its townscape rates among the finest in Europe, the streets and squares punctuated by spires and cupolas and dotted with leafy spaces. Its compact centre is ringed with village-like suburbs that retain their sense of identity, while the proximity of hills and sea adds to the city's beauty. With its face set confidently to the future as Scotland's longed-for autonomy becomes a fact, Edinburgh is experiencing a new sense of purpose and pride, making this a perfect time to enjoy its pleasures.

THE 10 ESSENTIALS

If you have only a limited period to enjoy Edinburgh, to ensure some unforgettable memories make time for at least a few of these.

- **Spend a leisurely morning** walking down the Royal Mile, making sure you explore its evocative wynds and closes to get a real sense of Edinburgh's history (➤ 24–5).
- **Seek out** one of Edinburgh's many vantage points to enjoy the full panorama of the city's superb setting – climb Arthur's Seat, stand on the Castle ramparts or walk up Calton Hill for some of the city's best views (➤ 16, 18, 35).
- **Take an open-air bus** ride around the city's main sights to get your bearings.
- **Take a couple of hours** to stroll around the Georgian splendour of the New Town, one of Europe's finest and most elegant examples of 18th-century town planning (➤ 21).
- **Relax in Princes Street Gardens**, where you can have lunch, catch a band concert, admire the Castle's silhouette and set your watch by the Floral Clock (➤ 59).
- **Head away from the centre** to hunt for presents and souvenirs in the enticing small shops in areas such as Stockbridge, the Grassmarket and Victoria Street (➤ 68, 47, 70).
- **Sample some Scottish food and drink** – specialities range from shortbread and haggis to Edinburgh rock and malt whisky, and you're bound to find something to enjoy.
- **Track down some local entertainment**; in summer choose from Festival events or the Tattoo, while in winter there's everything from Celtic Rock to Scottish pantomime.

- **Join the Saturday afternoon crowds** in Princes Street to get a feel for Edinburgh's people, then head for one of the smart café-bars in George Street (➤ 46).
- **Climb the Scott Monument** for views up and down Princes Street and across to the Mound and Castle (➤ 26).

Above: *the stirring sight of massed uniforms on the Esplanade below the floodlit castle*

Below: *a good view from the top deck on one of the frequent city sightseeing tours*

THE EDINBURGH CLASSIC TOUR

The Shaping of Edinburgh

c3000 BC
Area first settled by hunting tribes.

c1000 BC
First farmers are joined by immigrant Beaker People, who bring pottery and metal-working skills.

AD 78
Romans come north and defeat Calgacus.

c200 on
Departure of the Romans followed by waves of invading Angles, Britons, Vikings, and Scots from Ireland.

c950
MacAlpin kings repel Northumbrians, who have held southern Scotland for 300 years.

1018
Malcolm II defeats Northumbrians.

c1069
Malcolm III marries Margaret, sister of Edgar Atheling, heir to the English throne but usurped by William the Conqueror. Margaret lives on Castle Rock, where a chapel is built after her death.

1128
David I, Margaret's son, founds Abbey of Holyrood as a penance.

1314
Thomas Randolph retakes Edinburgh Castle from the English in name of Robert the Bruce.

1329
Edinburgh receives Royal Charter from Robert the Bruce.

1349
Black Death kills a third of population.

1435
St Antony's Chapel built on Arthur's Seat.

1457
James II decrees against the playing of 'futeball and golfe' as they interfere with archery practice.

1477
Charter granted by James III for markets to be held in the Grassmarket.

1498
Holyroodhouse built by James IV.

1513
James IV, and many citizens, killed at Battle of Flodden, construction begun on Flodden Wall for the defence of Edinburgh.

1544
Edinburgh attacked by English forces, who fail to take the city.

The Prince of Wales drives in the last rivet for the Forth Bridge

1566
David Rizzio, the favourite of Mary, Queen of Scots, murdered by Darnley and conspirators at Holyroodhouse.

1582
Townis College chartered; it later becomes Edinburgh University.

1603
James VI moves Court to London.

1633
Edinburgh officially becomes capital of Scotland.

1637
Tron Kirk built.

1638
Signing of the National Covenant, to defend the Scottish 'Kirk'.

10

1639
Parliament House built; used by Scottish Parliament until 1707.

1675
Physic Garden founded; forms nucleus of Royal Botanic Garden.

1695
Bank of Scotland chartered.

1692–8
Run of bad harvests leads to riots in the city.

1702–7
Scottish Parliament discusses, and finally ratifies, Act of Union, voting itself out of existence.

1736
The Porteous Riots.

1767
First plans for New Town adopted.

1769
Construction of Princes Street starts.

1770
Construction of Queen Street starts.

1771
Sir Walter Scott born in Edinburgh.

1787
First edition of Robert Burns' poems published.

1817
The Scotsman founded.

1824
Fire rages for three days in the High Street; as a result world's first municipal fire service is founded.

1832–50
Further construction of New Town.

1836
Waverley Station built.

1847
Alexander Graham Bell, the inventor of the telephone, born in Edinburgh.

1890
Forth Rail Bridge opened.

1895
Edinburgh is lit by electric street lighting.

1925
Murrayfield Stadium built for rugby matches.

1947
First Edinburgh International Festival.

1964
Heriot-Watt University founded.

1970
Commonwealth Pool and Meadowbank

Stadium built for Commonwealth Games held in same year.

1971
St James Centre opened and further demolition of Georgian houses in Princes Street.

1986
Commonwealth Games again held in Edinburgh.

1997
Referendum held to vote for return of Scottish Parliament.

1998
Site of new Scottish Parliament announced near Holyrood.

1999
Scottish Parliament sits for first time since 1707; construction of the Parliament building at Holyrood goes ahead.

The poet Robert Burns first came to Edinburgh in 1786

Peace & Quiet

Edinburgh is a busy, noisy city built on hills, and there will inevitably come a time when the footsore visitor seeks a respite from pavements, crowds and traffic fumes. The city is well-endowed with green and leafy spaces, and is uniquely blessed with a piece of true countryside right within the centre. Whether you're looking for a good strenuous walk, a gentle stroll or a shady bench, you'll find it somewhere.

Parks and Walks

Edinburgh's big parks include Holyrood Park (➤ 49), the Braid and Blackford Hills (➤ 34) and the Meadows (➤ 55), all good for walking and relaxing. Opposite the Meadows you'll find Bruntsfield Links, an open green space criss-crossed with paths and dotted with benches – a good place to relax and watch local children playing and cycling. If you want a peaceful walk, head for the Innocent Railway Walkway, which starts a little to the east and meanders between Holyrood Park and Prestonfield Golf Course to Duddingston (➤ 41). The old railway got its name from its accident-free record in the 19th century. Also on Edinburgh's south side you'll find the Union Canal, which linked Edinburgh, via the Forth and Clyde Canal, to Glasgow in the 19th century. The old towpath is rather

Swans are permanent residents at Duddingstone Loch, on the south side of Holyrood Park

down-at-heel, but is undergoing a major facelift as part of the city's Millennium Project. On the other side of the city, right at the northern edge of the New Town, lies Inverleith Park, which adjoins the lovely Royal Botanic Garden (➤ 23). This is a real family park, complete with children's swings and slides, a pond with ducks and swans to feed and numerous exuberant Edinburgh dogs enjoying an outing. In Inverleith's southeast corner you can gain access to the Water of Leith (➤ 70), an excellent walk which can be as long or short as you like. For saltwater breezes, head for Cramond foreshore (➤ 40) to the north, where a wide paved esplanade runs beside a shingly beach and the waters of the Firth of Forth, with pleasing views past Cramond Island to the hills of Fife.

Gardens

At first sight central Edinburgh seems rich in gardens, the New Town dotted with numerous green spaces amidst its squares and circuses. Sadly, these are all private and locked, keys being held by the owners of the surrounding properties. You can peer through the railings at these virtually empty gardens and enjoy them from a distance only. Head instead for Princes Street Gardens (➤ 59) and join the crowds of locals and visitors enjoying the colourful and immaculate flower beds. In the Old Town, you'll find Dunbar's Close Garden just off the bottom of the Canongate. This little-known 17th-century-style garden, trimly planted with box hedges and bright flowers, is a real refuge from the unrelenting cobbles of the Royal Mile. More tranquil still are some of Edinburgh's historic cemeteries, Greyfriars (➤ 48) being the most peaceful of all.

Inset: *Princes Street Gardens;* below: *Greyfriars Kirk*

Edinburgh's Famous

They all came from Edinburgh

It's impossible to visualise life without the telephone system, invented by Alexander Graham Bell, or operations without anaesthesia, pioneered by James Young Simpson. John Knox reformed Scotland's religion and Douglas Haig commanded armies for Britain. Robert Adam, Henry Raeburn and Allan Ramsay designed and decorated the city itself. World-wide, people have been entertained by the romances of Sir Walter Scott and the detective stories of Sir Arthur Conan Doyle.

Above: Mary, Queen of Scots, a romantic and tragic figure

Right: The Scottish author Robert Louis Stevenson
Below: Sean Connery, who demonstrates great enthusiasm for his native Scotland

Mary, Queen of Scots

Born in 1542, Mary became queen when she was six days old and was brought up in France. She married the Dauphin in 1558 but returned to Edinburgh on his death in 1561. This was a time of political and religious unrest, and Mary believed the English throne, held by Elizabeth, was hers by right. To further her claim she married Lord Darnley, murdered in 1567, by whom she had a son, the future James VI. Mary then married the Earl of Bothwell, despite his implication in Darnley's murder. Trapped by further intrigue and the machinations of her enemies, Mary finally abdicated and was executed by orders of her cousin, Elizabeth, in 1587.

Robert Louis Stevenson

The famous Scottish author was born in Edinburgh in 1850, a sickly child, who nevertheless later attended Edinburgh University and qualified as an advocate in 1875. Ill health forced him abroad, and his travels both inspired his early books and led to his meeting with his future wife, an American divorcée 10 years his senior. Most of his best-loved works date from after their marriage, including *Treasure Island* and *Kidnapped*. In 1890 he settled in Samoa, where his health improved, and he was writing at the height of his mature powers when he unexpectedly died in 1894.

Sean Connery

The future James Bond drifted through various jobs, most famously that of a milkman, after leaving school, aged 13, in 1943. His first break saw him in the chorus of *South Pacific*, and his big chance came when he was cast as Ian Fleming's hero in the film version of *Dr No* in 1962. Now one of the cinema's major and most highly paid stars, Connery has long since left Edinburgh, though still remaining apparently loyal to his Scottish roots.

Top Ten

Above: *fireworks light up the sky at
the Edinburgh Festival*
Right: *traditional Highland
dress*

1
Arthur's Seat

Edinburgh is unique in Europe in possessing a craggy peak within a stone's throw of the city centre, the perfect antidote to crowds and culture.

Holyrood Park (➤ 49) and Edinburgh itself are dominated by the extinct volcano known as Arthur's Seat, soaring to 251m above the city. The volcano erupted some 325 million years ago during the early Carboniferous era; its other remnants make up the Castle Rock and Calton Hill (➤ 35). Keen geologists can trace the various stages of today's rock formations – the summit marks where the cone erupted, while molten rocks formed the sills such as Salisbury Crags and Samson's Ribs. Erosion during the Ice Age laid bare the inside of the volcano, isolating the twin peaks of Arthur's Seat and the Crow Hill. Explanations for the name vary; some believe it to be a corruption of the Gaelic name for 'archers', others claim the Normans associated it with the semi-mythical King Arthur.

You can climb Arthur's Seat from a path starting near St Margaret's Well just inside the Palace of Holyroodhouse entrance to the park; the path divides at the start of Hunter's Bog valley and either branch leads to the summit. Take the right hand one to go along the path called the Radical Road, which runs directly beneath the rockface of Salisbury Crags, or the left, through the Dasses, to the top. Easiest of all is to drive to the car park near Dunsapie Loch; from here it's a short, steepish climb to the top, with one or two rocky scrambles to give you a feeling of real achievement. However you get there, it's worth it for the panorama of the city, the Firth of Forth, the Pentland Hills and the coastline east of Edinburgh.

✝ 29F2

✉ Holyrood Park

☎ 0131 556 3407

🕐 24 hours, 365 days a year, but no vehicular access to Dunsapie Loch on Sun

🚌 1, 6, 36, 69, 85

♿ Few

✋ Free

↔ Dynamic Earth (➤ 17); Palace of Holyroodhouse (➤ 22); Royal Mile (➤ 24–5); Duddingston (➤ 41); Holyrood Abbey (➤ 49); Holyrood Park (➤ 49)

Above: *looking across to Arthur's Seat from the Royal Observatory*
Right: *glorious views from the summit make the climb worth while*

16

2
Dynamic Earth

Edinburgh's Millennium Landmark project has brought a state-of-the-art attraction to Holyrood, the heart of devolved Scotland.

Against the backdrop of Salisbury Crags rises a light and airy structure, with a translucent spiked and tented roof, fronted by a sweeping stone amphitheatre. This is Dynamic Earth, a geological visitors' centre telling the story of our planet using special effects and the latest in interactive technology.

A visit to Dynamic Earth lasts around 90 minutes and first concentrates on the creation of life; a 'time machine' takes you back to witness meteor showers, followed by the image of a barren, newly formed planet. Volcanoes erupt, the earth moves and shakes, sulphurous smells are all around. Next comes the Ice Age, as you experience a virtual-reality helicopter trip through frozen wastes. Other areas concentrate on the evolution of life, the oceans, the polar regions (complete with a genuine, and growing, iceberg), tundra and temperate climatic zones. Next comes a visit to a tropical rainforest, where the air is damp and full of squawks and chatters of unseen animals and birds. Every 15 minutes the sky darkens, lightning flashes, thunder roars and sheets of torrential rain pour down. Leaving here, you enter a huge domed space, the climax of the visit, with a dazzling series of images showing the beauty and power of our ever-changing world.

There are plenty of interactive computer programmes and information boards for younger children. There are dinosaurs and dodos, a submarine 'trip' to view ocean life, giant screens showing the glowing colours of the Northern Lights and much information on ecology, all presented with the emphasis very much on learning through fun.

✚ 29F3

✉ William Younger Centre, Holyrood

☎ 0131 550 7800

🕐 Apr–Oct daily 10–6; Nov–Mar Wed–Sun 10–5. Closed 24, 25 Dec

🚌 1, 6

🍴 Restaurant (££)

♿ Excellent

✋ Expensive

↔ Arthur's Seat (➤ 16); Palace of Holyroodhouse (➤ 22); Royal Mile (➤ 24–5); Holyrood Abbey (➤ 49); Holyrood Park (➤ 49)

Left and above: *children and adults take time to enjoy the excellent sea life displays*

3
Edinburgh Castle

📍 28C2

✉ Edinburgh Castle, Castle Hill

☎ 0131 225 9846

🕐 Apr–Sep 9:30–6; Oct–Mar 9:30–5. Closed 25, 26 Dec; check for New Year times

🍴 Restaurant and café (£–££)

🚌 23, 27, 34, 35

♿ Few

✋ Very expensive

↔ Edinburgh Castle Museums (► 44); Royal Mile (► 24–5)

❓ Four-hour audio guide included in entry price. Edinburgh Military Tattoo held on Castle Esplanade, Aug

Tourists enjoying the sunshine in the courtyard at Edinburgh Castle

Redolent with 1,000 years of history, the courtyards and buildings of Edinburgh's main tourist attraction live up to its dominant position.

Edinburgh Castle rises from an extinct volcanic outcrop at the top of the Royal Mile. From the sweep of the Esplanade, used each August for the famous Military Tattoo, the 19th-century Gatehouse gives access to the heart of the castle complex. The oldest building is the 12th-century St Margaret's Chapel, built by David I in memory of his mother, on the highest point of the Castle Rock. Around and below the chapel are the defensive batteries, and buildings such as the 1742 Governor's House, still used as the Governor's official residence, the superb Great Hall with its hammerbeam roof, and the Palace Block, a royal palace from the time of James I. Here, in 1566, Mary, Queen of Scots gave birth to James VI, who was to become James I of England. The Scottish Crown Jewels, the oldest royal regalia in Britain, are the centrepiece of an exhibition telling their story and that of the Stone of Destiny, recently returned to Scotland from Westminster Abbey, where it had lain since Edward I took it south in 1296.

Leave time to explore the vaults known as the French Prisons below the Great Hall; the name recalls their use during the Napoleonic Wars. Here you'll find the massive siege gun known as Mons Meg, which was given to James II in 1457 and could fire a 267kg stone nearly 3km. Today, the only gun fired regularly from the castle is the 1 o'clock gun (► 52), echoing from the Mills Mount Battery.

4
Museum of Scotland

An eye-catching modern building houses over 10,000 objects telling the story of Scotland's history, people, culture and achievements.

✚ 29D2

✉ Chambers Street

☎ 0131 225 7534/247 4219

🕐 Wed–Sat and Mon, 10–5; Tue 10–8; Sun 12–5. Closed 25 Dec

🍴 Tower Restaurant; ☎ 0131 225 3003 🕐 Mon–Sat 10–11pm, Sun 12–11pm (££–£££)

🚌 7, 14, 28, 45

♿ Excellent

👐 Moderate (free on Tue 4:30–8)

↔ Cowgate (➤ 39); Greyfriars Kirk (➤ 48)

❓ Regular lunchtime lectures; guided general and themed tours; free portable sound guides; cinema (The Lumière, ☎ 0131 247 4219 🕐 Fri, Sat, Sun) showing wide range of British and foreign old and new films (➤ 110)

Above: *the museum's exterior is reminiscent of a fortified tower*

The Museum of Scotland opened in 1998 as an extension of the old Royal Museum, itself a fine mixed collection of natural history and the decorative arts, housed in a Victorian building embellished with splendid cast-iron work. A new national museum for Scotland had been mooted since the early 1950s, and the finished complex provides the perfect foil for the superb collections within.

The museum is divided into seven main sections, each concentrating on a theme in the development of Scotland, and illustrating this through exhibits, display boards, and interactive information. From the geological formation of the landscape move on to wildlife and historical and modern land use, then to a section on early people, where a striking group of sculptures by Eduardo Paolozzi is decked with ancient jewellery and artefacts. The next level looks at the Kingdom of the Scots, the years between 900 and 1701, when Scotland was an independent nation with a full cultural, social and religious life. Here you'll find the famous Lewis chess-pieces, carved from whalebone in the 12th century, the 8th-century Monymusk Reliquary, and the Bute Mazer, probaby made for Robert the Bruce. Later treasures include fine Scottish silver, glass and textiles. Moving on through displays showing the country's development after the Union until the Industrial Revolution, you come to the industries that made 19th-century Scotland 'the workshop of the world'. Leave time for the top floor: devoted to the 20th century, it's crammed with objects chosen by the Scottish public as being representative of the present age – everything from an automatic washing machine to a disposable syringe.

5
National Gallery of Scotland

Superb Old Master and Scottish paintings, displayed in sumptuously decorated galleries, make the National Gallery a draw for all visitors.

✚ 28C3

✉ The Mound

☎ 0131 624 6200; recorded information 0131 332 2266

🕐 Mon–Sat 10–5; Sun 2–5. Closed 25 Dec

🍴 Café £

🚌 4, 21, 24, 63

♿ Excellent but no access to room A1

✋ Free

↔ The Mound (► 56); Princes Street (► 59); Princes Street Gardens (► 59); Royal Scottish Academy (► 61); Scott Monument (► 26)

❓ Lectures and changing exhibitions; see Bulletin of the National Galleries of Scotland, published bi-monthly and available from the gallery

Perhaps the greatest charm of the National Gallery of Scotland is its size, for this comprehensive and high-quality collection can be enjoyed in a leisurely hour or two. Housed in a splendid classical revival building designed by William Playfair in 1848, it spans the history of European painting from the Italian Renaissance to French Impressionism. Many rooms are decorated to Playfair's original colour scheme, and contain fine examples of furniture contemporary with the artistic movements.

Italian Renaissance pictures include a lovely *Madonna and Child* by Verrocchio and Raphael's *Bridgwater Madonna*, part of the Duke of Sutherland's collection. The loan of this painting in 1946 helped give the National Gallery international significance. Northern Renaissance pictures includes Hugo van der Goes' Trinity altarpiece, commissioned in the 15th century for an Edinburgh church. Titian and Tintoretto represent Venice, El Greco and Velazquez Spain – look out for the superb and tactile picture entitled *An Old Woman Cooking Eggs*, where you can practically feel the egg shell. Works by French artists include Poussin's cerebral and detached cycle of the Seven Sacraments, and some superb Impressionist pictures glowing with light. There are also German, Flemish and Dutch works, all of great quality.

Leave time to enjoy the Scottish collection, housed in an underground extension, built in the 1970s. This concentrates mainly on 18th- and 19th-century artists such as Allan Ramsay, David Wilkie and Henry Raeburn; the latter's engaging portrait, *The Reverend Robert Walker Skating*, is among the gallery's most popular pictures.

Below: *the rich original colours of the gallery's interior are a perfect foil for its treasures* (right)

6
The New Town

One of Europe's greatest examples of Georgian town planning, the New Town combines crescents, squares and circuses into a harmonious whole.

Elegant façades and balanced design sum up New Town architecture

By the mid 18th century the crowded tenements and narrow streets of old Edinburgh were no longer adequate to house the population and institutions of the burgeoning city. A competition was launched with a view to building a fine 'New Town' to the north; the winning design was by James Craig and construction began in 1767. The Nor' Loch, on the site of Princes Street Gardens (➤ 59) was drained, and the North Bridge built to link the Old Town with the new. The first stage comprised three symmetrical streets, George, Queen and Princes (➤ 46, 60, 59), linking St Andrew and Charlotte Squares (➤ 63, 36), the triumphant façades of the latter designed by Robert Adam in 1791. The more prosperous citizens flocked to live here necessitating further development. Robert Reid, William Playfair and James Gillespie Graham laid out the magnificent streets around Great King Street, the Royal Circus and Moray Place, a highly successful amalgam of interlinking crescents, octagons and ovals. This was followed between 1817 and 1860 by the construction of the West End, centring around Melville Crescent.

The result is the world's largest Georgian city development, with over 11,000 listed properties. Happily, despite the appalling redevelopment of Princes Street in the 1960s, most has remained untouched. More than three-quarters of New Town houses are still in residential use, making the entire area an unchanged enclave.

➕ 28B3

✉ The New Town

🍴 Restaurants, bars, pubs and cafés throughout the area (£–£££)

🚌 13, 27, 35, 80

♿ Good

✋ Free

🔄 Charlotte Square (➤ 36); George Street (➤ 46); The Georgian House (➤ 46); Hanover Street (➤ 48); Princes Street (➤ 59); Queen Street (➤ 60); St Andrew Square (➤ 63)

7
Palace of Holyroodhouse

The slopes of Arthur's Seat rise up behind the palace

The Queen's official Scottish residence, set against the background of Arthur's Seat, stands at the eastern end of the historic Royal Mile.

 29F3

 0131 556 7371;
recorded information
0131 556 1096

Apr–Oct 9:30–5:15;
Nov–Mar 9:30–3:45;
closed Good Friday, 2
weeks early May, early
Jun, late Jun to mid-Jul
and 25–26 Dec.
As the palace is a
royal residence,
opening times may be
subject to change at
short notice – please
telephone to check

 1, 6

 Good

 Expensive

 Arthur's Seat (➤ 16);
Dynamic Earth (➤ 17);
Holyrood Abbey (➤ 49);
Holyrood Park (➤ 49);
Royal Mile (➤ 24–5)

Winter exhibitions from
the Royal Collections,
Nov–Mar

The Palace of Holyroodhouse stands on the site of the original guest house for the medieval Holyrood Abbey, and is used today by Queen Elizabeth II as her home and office whenever she is in Edinburgh.

In 1501 James IV built a four-storey corner tower with gabled roof and balustrade, the existing northwest tower. Later additions were damaged and burned in 1544 and again in 1650. The palace attained its present form in 1671, when William Bruce designed an Italian-style courtyard quadrangle around which he built today's elegant structure. He fronted it by a tower matching the surviving medieval one, to which it is linked by a grand entrance screen. The State Apartments lie on the south side of the courtyard, a suite of grand rooms including the Royal Dining Room, the Morning Drawing Room and the Throne Room. Across the court, the north range contains the Picture Gallery, decorated with portraits of 111 Scottish kings and queens from King Fergus in the 4th century to James VII, imaginatively created to order by Jacob de Wet. Holyroodhouse has historical associations with many monarchs, among them James II, James IV and Charles II (whose canopied bed is on show), while Bonnie Prince Charlie held receptions here in the heady early days of the 1745 Jacobite Uprising. The memory of Mary Queen of Scots is perhaps the most vivid; it was in her second-floor rooms that her Italian favourite, David Rizzio, was stabbed in 1566 by her second husband, Lord Darnley, and his fellow conspirators.

8
Royal Botanic Garden

The Royal Botanic Garden's collections of trees, shrubs and flowers are an oasis of quiet, and draw plantsmen and garden lovers from many countries.

Lush aquatic vegetation in one of the glasshouses

The Royal Botanic Garden started life in 1670 with the founding of a Physic Garden near the Palace of Holyrood-house; three centuries later the garden is a thriving and internationally famous plant study centre, and a haven of colour and scent throughout the year.

Moved to its present site in 1823, the garden covers 28 ha of undulating ground lying between the city centre and the Firth of Forth. Winding paths link the different sections of the garden, much of which is grassed and dotted with the superb trees which comprise the Arboretum, a collection of more than 2000 tree species, carpeted in spring with delicate spreads of bulbs. Spring flowers give way to the blazing colours of rhododendrons and azaleas, their flaming reds and yellows offset by underplanting of lilies, primulas and *meconopsis*. The Rock Garden is at its best in late spring, its rocky slopes brilliant with alpine and Mediterranean plants, while near by the Heath Garden has year-round displays of Scottish and other heathers. High summer sees the 165m-long herbaceous border, with its stately beech hedge, at its best, and the rose collections fill the air with scent. Horticulturalists will be fascinated by the Chinese garden, where wild plants clothe the slopes of a watery ravine leading to a tranquil pond.

The garden is particularly famous for its glasshouses, a complex of ten contrasting structures where you'll find everything from Amazonian rainforest plants to cacti from deserts all over the world. Don't miss the Temperate Palm House, an elegant cast-iron structure built in 1858, and still the tallest in Britain.

✚ 28B4

✉ 20A Inverleith Row

☎ 0131 552 7171

🕐 Apr–Aug 9:30–7; Sep 9:30–6; Oct, Feb–Mar 9:30–5; Nov–Jan 9:30–4

🍴 Café and snack-bar (£–££)

🚌 8, 19, 23, 27

♿ Very good

🎟 Free

↔ The Colonies (➤ 37); Stockbridge (➤ 68); Water of Leith (➤ 70)

9

The Royal Mile

🕇 29E3

✉ The Royal Mile

🍴 Restaurants, bars, pubs and cafés throughout the area (£–£££)

🚌 1, 6, 27, 45

♿ Good

✋ Free

Below: the highlights of the Royal Mile are many and varied

The Royal Mile runs downhill from Edinburgh Castle to Holyrood Palace and provides a focal point in the Old Town.

The colourful, noisy streets of the Royal Mile are the tourist hub of Edinburgh. Thronged with people, lined with medieval tenements, packed with gift shops, and frequently echoing to the sounds of the pipes, this is the first port of call for every visitor. From the main thoroughfare, enticing closes, wynds and vennels lead off between the buildings; discovering these is an essential part of exploring the Mile. Start at the top, where the solid bulk of the castle stands above the Esplanade with its splendid views, and work your way down to Holyrood, the historic full stop to an area crammed with history and atmosphere, described by Daniel Defoe as 'the largest, longest and finest street … in the world'.

The Royal Mile, its various sections known by different names, is the oldest part of Edinburgh. It developed in the Middle Ages along the ridge sloping down from the castle. It was enclosed by the city walls, which resulted in buildings growing ever higher as the population expanded. Steep slopes descend on either side of the ridge, so buildings which are only a few storeys tall on the High Street side can tower on the other side, producing the striking silhouette seen from Princes Street. These tenements, known as 'lands', housed a complete cross-section of Edinburgh society. Sanitation was virtually non-existent, household waste being flung out of the windows with a cry of 'gardey loo', a corruption of the French words *gardez l'eau*. Conditions and overcrowding worsened over the centuries, plague and fire were frequent, and in the 1770s, as construction of the New Town (► 21) forged ahead, the upper classes moved out.

Starting from the Esplanade look out for Ramsay Gardens at the top of Castlehill. This splendid 18th-century baronial complex was built by the poet Allan Ramsay. Past the Tolbooth St John's Kirk, now the Edinburgh Festival Hub (➤ 45), fine 16th- and 17th-century tenements line the Lawnmarket (➤ 51); Dr Johnson visited James Boswell in James' Court just off here. Another nearby close was home to Deacon Brodie, a city worthy who led a double life as a burglar. He was hanged outside St Giles' Cathedral (➤ 64), which stands at the top of the High Street section. Near here, Edinburgh's last public hanging took place in 1864, while opposite the cathedral the City Chambers stand on the site of Mary King's Close, a medieval street which was blocked off during the Great Plague of 1645, its inhabitants left to die. Further down, there are more fine 16th-century buildings and a pub, the World's End, whose name commemorates the old city boundary. Below the High Street the Mile becomes Canongate, named after the Augustinian monks whose monastery once stood here. High points include Canongate Kirk, a serene Dutch-inspired building dating from 1688; Mary, Queen of Scots' secretary, David Rizzio, is buried in the churchyard, along with the economist Adam Smith (1723–90). More attractive old houses line the bottom end of Canongate, which widens slightly to bring you to the gates of the Palace of Holyroodhouse (➤ 22).

Looking down the Royal Mile from the High Street towards the Canongate

10
Scott Monument

Fine views to the castle and Princes Street from one of the most grandiose memorials to a writer ever built make the climb well worth while.

✚ 29D3

✉ East Princes Street Gardens

☎ 0131 529 4068/3993

🕓 Mar–May and Oct, daily 10–6; Jun–Sep Mon–Sat 9–8, Sun 10–6; Nov–Feb 10–4

🍴 Refreshment kiosk in East Princes Gardens (£)

🚌 3, 11, 21 44

♿ moderate

↔ National Gallery of Scotland (➤ 20); Calton Hill (➤ 35); Hanover Street (➤ 48); The Mound (➤ 56); Princes Street (➤ 59); Princes Street Gardens (➤ 59); Register House (➤ 60) Royal Scottish Academy (➤ 61); Waverley Market (➤ 71)

Worn out with excessive work in an attempt to pay off his creditors and those of his bankrupt publishers and printers, Sir Walter Scott died at his home, Abbotsford (➤ 77), in 1832. He was regarded by his contemporaries as one of Scotland's greatest writers, and no time was lost in erecting a fitting monument to his genius. The architect was George Meikle Kemp, a self-taught draughtsman, who won a competition for the memorial's design in 1838. The 61m-high monument went up between 1840 and 1846, a riot of ornate Gothicism with a seated statue of Scott beneath the central vault. In contrast to the sandstone of the building, the statue is carved from white Carrara marble, the block from which it was sculpted happily having survived falling into Livorno harbour on its way from Italy to Leith. Scott is shown draped in a plaid, with his favourite deerhound, Maida. The monument's 64 niches contain statues that represent many of the characters from Scott's works – fans of the Waverley novels can identify their favourites.

Climb right to the top of the Monument for sweeping views over the city centre; the ticket price includes a certificate to prove that you really did it. If the prospect of the 287 steps seems rather daunting, you could go as far as the first level only. Here you'll find a small room that displays information about Scott's life and work, and there are also headphones which you can use to listen to readings and musical settings of his novels.

The pinnacles of the Scott Monument rise above colourful summer flowerbeds

What to See

Above: the famous Murrayfield Stadium
Right: an old street sign in Huntly House Museum

27

EDINBURGH

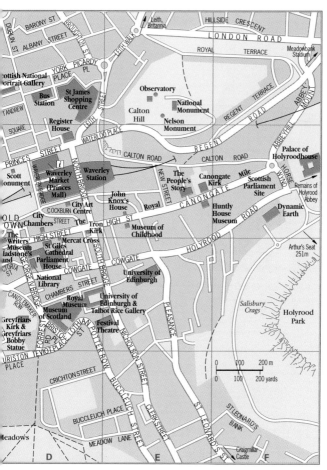

A range of tartan ties on display in a souvenir shop

Edinburgh

For many Scots, the Edinburgh of today seems more like a true capital city than it has for almost three hundred years, since it is now the centre where the Scottish Parliament sits to determine issues affecting the country's people.

The city has boasted wonderful architecture and fine musems for many years; as it faces the third millennium it does so with a sound economy, growing prosperity and a clutch of new buildings and enterprises. It offers excellent exhibition and conference facilities, its financial institutions are of international importance and the research carried out in its universities is renowned world-wide. Increasingly a truly cosmopolitan city, with a cultural life whose dynamism is no longer confined to August, Edinburgh rates highly for the quality of life enjoyed by its citizens and those who come to visit.

'The impression Edinburgh has made upon us is very great; it is quite beautiful, totally unlike anything else I have seen......'

QUEEN VICTORIA,
2 September 1842.
*Leaves from the Journal of Our Life
in the Highlands*

———————●———————

The lights of the Balmoral Hotel glow in competition with an autumn sunset

Exploring Edinburgh

The best way to explore Edinburgh is on foot. You need to do this to experience the true feel of the city, for no bus will transport you down the narrow medieval closes of old Edinburgh or through the quiet and spacious residential streets of the New Town. Go where your fancy takes you and discover the hidden corners which do so much to make this one of Europe's truly great cities.

Above: *there are plenty of maps and tourist information leaflets to help you get the best from your stay*

Below: *you may need to buy one of these, but at least it will remind you of your visit to Scotland*

Unlike many capitals, Edinburgh is small enough to allow you to do this, though you may want to take a bus before starting your day's wanderings, and a taxi at the end of a footsore day, when the fact that Edinburgh is a hilly city is only too apparent. Concentrate on one area at a time – this is easy to do with the city so conveniently divided into the Old and New Towns. Spend time too, venturing out from the centre to Stockbridge, Duddingston, sea-shore Cramond and the buzzing waterfront areas of Leith. They all have their own characteristics and charm, as well as tourist sights which you won't want to miss. Explore Edinburgh's parks, too, for few other cities can boast such a variety, from the genuine countryside of Holyrood Park to the manicured lawns and bright flowerbeds of the Royal Botanic Garden.

As in any large city, Edinburgh has its poorer areas, especially on the big outer estates; they're best avoided by visitors, as are the Meadows and dockside Leith at night.

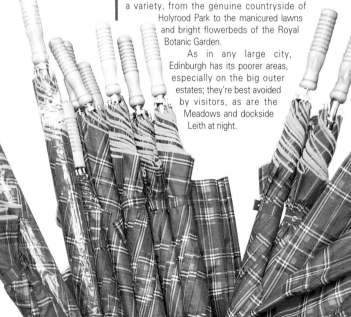

ANN STREET ✪

The early 19th-century construction of the Raeburn Estate, built between the New Town (► 21) and Stockbridge (► 68), was instrumental in bringing new wealth down the hill as the rich moved in, occupying streets such as Ann Street. Now one of Edinburgh's most exclusive addresses, its charm lies in its scale, almost miniature compared to the grandeur of the New Town. Each house in this classically inspired terrace of perfectly proportioned houses is fronted by a garden, producing a beguiling mix of small-scale architectural splendour and cottagey charm.

✚ 28A4
✉ Ann Street
🚌 19, 40, 55, 81
♿ Good
↔ New Town (► 21)

ARTHUR'S SEAT (► 16, TOP TEN)

ASSEMBLY HALL ✪✪

The temporary home of the Scottish Parliament (► 66), the Assembly Hall was designed by David Bryce and built between 1858 and 1859 to house the General Assembly of the Free Church of Scotland, a splinter group that broke away from the established Church of Scotland in 1843. The complex was deliberately designed to frame the spire of the Tolbooth Church behind, while the gatehouse towers are sited on the axis of the Royal Academy further down the Mound.

✚ 28C2
✉ Mound Place, but public entrance: Mylne's Court, Lawnmarket, Royal Mile
☎ 0845 278 1999/0131 348 5000
🕐 Debating Chamber open during parliamentary sessions (Wed AM; all day Thu)
🚌 1, 6, 27, 45
♿ Excellent
✋ Free
↔ Royal Mile (► 24–5); The Lawnmarket (► 51)

The beautiful chandeliers in the grand Hall of the Assembly Rooms

ASSEMBLY ROOMS ✪

Even if you're not attending a concert, the Assembly Rooms, opened in 1787, are well worth a quick visit. The plain façade, with its massive 1818 portico, leads to a series of elegantly proportioned rooms planned for equally elegant social occasions. The ballroom, 28m long and over 13m wide, is lit by dazzling chandeliers; the music hall, even larger, is equally impressive. Since the 1940s the Assembly Rooms have been a key festival venue.

✚ 28C3
✉ 54 George Street
☎ 0131 220 4349/220 4348
🕐 Mon–Sat 10–5
🚌 19, 23, 40, 45
♿ Good
✋ Varies for performances
↔ George Street (► 46)

Above: *the city and
surrounding countryside
from Blackford Hill*
Right: *the Royal
Observatory's telescope
puts visitors into
perspective*

BLACKFORD HILL ✪

Blackford Hill, south of the city centre, is seen at its best on uncrowded weekdays, and is a good place to head for an afternoon's fresh air and exercise and some splendid city views. Its 164m summit is an easy climb from the surrounding parkland, up grassy slopes covered with bright yellow gorse. From here, the green southern suburbs stretch north, with Arthur's Seat over to the right and Edinburgh Castle ahead. You'll also find the Royal Observatory (➤ 61) on Blackford Hill. Head downhill to the wooded path that winds beside the Braid Burn to a castellated 18th-century villa known as the Hermitage of Braid. It is now a countryside information centre which will fill you in on the surprisingly wide range of wildlife to be found in the area.

BRAID HILLS ✪✪

If you're feeling energetic, you could combine a walk on Blackford Hill with a few more miles over the Braid Hills (205m) which lie just to the south and are linked to Blackford by good paths. Much of the area is covered by golf courses (➤ 114); these were laid out by the City of Edinburgh in 1889 as public courses when play on city-centre Bruntsfield Links was becoming restricted. Few tourists penetrate these outer hills, outliers of the Pentlands, and the only people you're likely to meet are local golfers and dog-walkers. There are more sweeping panoramas from Braid; on a clear day look north and to your left for a fine view of the Forth Bridges.

CALTON HILL ✪✪✪

A clutch of remarkable monuments adorns the slopes of Calton Hill (108m), another remnant of the volcano which formed Edinburgh's geological structure. The view from the hill's summit is splendid, with all Edinburgh spreading around and sweeping vistas down the coast and across to Fife. For even wider views, climb the 143 steps to the top of **Nelson Monument**, built in 1807, and housing a timepiece in the shape of a white ball which drops from a mast each day at 1PM. Next to it looms the unfinished National Monument; modelled on the Parthenon in Athens, it was intended as a memorial to the Scots who fell in the Napoleonic Wars. Only twelve columns had been completed when the money ran out and it was known for years as 'Edinburgh's Disgrace'. The City Observatory, with its Gothic tower and astronomical dome, stands near by; the grandiose Playfair Monument commemorates John Playfair, first president of the Astronomical Institution.

➕ 29E4
✉ Calton Hill
🚌 26, 33, 40, 85
♿ Few
↔ Waterloo Place (➤ 71)

Nelson Monument

✉ Calton Hill
☎ 0131 556 2716
🕐 Apr–Sep, Mon 1–6, Tue–Sat 10–6; Oct–Mar, Mon–Sat 10–3
🚌 26, 33, 40, 85
💷 Moderate
↔ Waterloo Place (➤ 71)

CAMERA OBSCURA ✪✪

When the camera obscura was invented in the 19th century it must have seemed magical to be able to view the moving scene outside from within a darkened building. The device uses mirrors to project images of the outside world on to lenses and thus to a white disk. The lenses rotate through 360°, giving you a bird's-eye view of the surroundings. It's a fair climb up to Edinburgh's Camera Obscura, but you can pause at the hologram exhibition to get your breath. Choose a clear day for your visit; the camera depends on natural light and you won't see much if it's gloomy.

➕ 28C2
✉ Castlehill, Royal Mile
☎ 0131 226 3709
🕐 Apr–Oct, daily 9:30–6 (later in high summer); Nov–Mar, 10–5
🚌 23, 27, 34, 35
💷 Expensive
↔ Edinburgh Castle (➤ 18); Scotch Whisky Heritage Centre (➤ 65); Royal Mile (➤ 24–5)

DID YOU KNOW?

The tower of the Balmoral Hotel, at the east end of Princes Street, is embellished with a fine four-sided clock. For over 100 years this has been kept a few minutes fast, to help the travelling public catch their trains in nearby Waverley Station on time.

✚ 28B3
✉ Charlotte Square
🍴 Restaurants, bars and
cafés near by (£–££)
🚌 12, 22, 33, 51
♿ Very good
↔ George Street (➤ 46);
The Georgian House
(➤ 46); Princes Street
(➤ 59); Princes Street
Gardens (➤ 59); Queen
Street (➤ 60)

*There's plenty to buy as
well as to admire in the
City Art Centre*

CHARLOTTE SQUARE ⊙⊙

Charlotte Square, named after Queen Charlotte, wife of George III, was designed by Robert Adam in 1791 as part of the First New Town (➤ 21). This triumphant and harmonious example of symmetrical architecture, with its central garden, was planned to balance St Andrew Square at the other end of George Street. The north and south sides of the square present an unbroken façade which hides the blocks' 11 individual houses. The west side is occupied by West Register House, originally St George's Church, an impressive porticoed building topped by a cupola. The square was intended for residential purposes, though today many of the buildings house offices. If you want a glimpse of 18th-century life head for the Georgian House (➤ 46) on the north side.

✚ 29D3
✉ 2 Market Street
☎ 0131 529 3993
🕐 Mon–Sat 10–5, Sundays
during Edinburgh Festival
2–5
🍴 Restaurant and café
(£–££)
🚌 2, 12, 25, 36, 43, 80
♿ Very good
🎫 Free, but charge for
entrance to major
temporary exhibitions
↔ Scott Monument (➤ 26);
Waverley Market (Princes
Mall) (➤ 71)

CITY ART CENTRE ⊙

The City Art Centre was established in 1980 in a building originally constructed in 1899 as part of the *The Scotsman* newspape's offices, a splendid baroque edifice with an imaginatively converted interior. Its six galleries house the city's collection of Scottish art and provide space for a diverse range of temporary exhibitions. Edinburgh has a policy of providing 'something for everyone', and you're as likely to find a show devoted to *Star Trek* as to Michelangelo drawings or Egyptian antiquities. The permanent collection includes paintings, watercolours, photographs and sculpture. Look out for works by William MacTaggart, J P Fergusson and Anne Redpath, all important 20th-century Edinburgh artists and members of the school known as the Scottish Colourists.

THE COLONIES ✪✪

Downstream from the Stock Bridge, the Water of Leith walkway (➤ 70) will lead to you to one of Edinburgh's more picturesque corners, a cluster of streets of artisans' houses tucked away at the foot of the New Town heights. Here you will find the 11 parallel rows of terraced houses known as The Colonies, running at right angles to the Water of Leith. This development was constructed by the Edinburgh Co-Operative Building Company in 1861 for local workmen and their families. Each house is divided into upper and lower dwellings, with outside stairs to the top flats and tiny gardens. Many houses are decorated with plaques depicting the tools used by the tradesmen involved in their construction – masons, plumbers, joiners, plasterers and decorators.

✚ 28B4
✉ Stockbridge
🚌 19, 20, 28, 34
♿ Good
🔄 Stockbridge (➤ 68)

Signs of family life are still evident outside the charming terraces of The Colonies

CORSTORPHINE ✪

Once a farming village on the road to Glasgow, Corstorphine is a mainly residential district, which you see if you visit Edinburgh Zoo (➤ 45) on the slopes of Corstorphine Hill. You can walk to the summit (162m), which is crowned by Clermiston Tower, erected in 1871 to commemorate the centenary of the birth of Sir Walter Scott. South of the main Glasgow road lies the heart of old Corstorphine, with a pleasant church and barrel-shaped dovecote for 1,060 birds, once serving the long-vanished castle. Near by stands the massive Corstorphine Sycamore, said to have been brought as a sapling from the East in the 15th century and haunted by the ghost of Christian Nimmo, who stabbed her lover, James Lord Forrester, under its branches in 1679.

✚ 79D3
🚌 1, 12, 26, 32
♿ Good
🔄 Edinburgh Zoo (➤ 45)

The Royal Mile

Start at the Castle Esplanade and head down Castlehill passing the Scotch Whisky Heritage Centre (➤ 65) on your right and the Camera Obscura (➤ 35) on your left. Continue to the Tolbooth Church, now the Edinburgh Festival Hub (➤ 45), and cross the road into The Lawnmarket (➤ 51).

Distance
1.8km/1.1 miles

Time
30 minutes without stops, 3–6 hours with museum visits

Start Point
Castle Esplanade
✚ 28C2
🚌 1, 6, 28, 40, 45

End Point
Palace of Holyroodhouse
✚ 29F3
🚌 1, 6

Lunch
Common Grounds (£–££)
✉ 2/3 North Bank Street
☎ 0131 226 1416

John Knox's House

Wander through some of the quiet closes leading off the Lawnmarket to escape the crowds and soak up the 200-year-old atmosphere.

Cross the street at the junction where The Lawnmarket becomes the High Street and is bisected by North Bank Street and George IV Bridge.

The ornate domed building at the bottom of the slope to your left is the headquarters of the Bank of Scotland, first built in 1802 and re-designed by David Bryce in 1864.

Continue downhill, passing Parliament Square (➤ 58) and St Giles Cathedral (➤ 64) on your right.

Opposite the Cathedral, an impressive Edwardian baroque complex houses the City Chambers, mainly built between 1898 and 1904.

Continue to the Tron Kirk (➤ 69) on the corner of the Bridges. Cross the road and walk down to the bottom of the High Street and cross St Mary's Street into the Canongate stretch.

You'll find the Museum of Childhood (➤ 57) and John Knox's House (➤ 50) as you approach the end of the High Street.

Walk down the Canongate.

This stretch has the Huntly House and People's Story museums (➤ 50 and 58). At the bottom notice the attractive houses with crow-stepped gables.

Cross Abbey Strand to reach the gates of the Palace of Holyroodhouse (➤ 22).

COWGATE ✪

The long gloomy street called the Cowgate runs canyon-like beneath the South and George IV bridges, and connects The Grassmarket (➤ 47) with the Canongate area of the Old Town. Through here, in medieval times, cattle were driven from the plots behind the High Street houses to pasture outside the walls. By 1500 the Cowgate had become Edinburgh's first fashionable suburb, lined with the houses of rich merchants and the aristocracy. Centuries later, it housed Edinburgh's large Irish community and was home to the city's breweries. Look out for **St Cecilia's Hall**; built in 1763, this was the city's first concert venue. The Holyrood Project, a massive development scheme comprising the new Scottish Parliament and other buildings, and the opening of new bars and clubs are together revitalising this area.

➕ 29D2
✉ Cowgate
🚌 1, 28 40
♿ Good
↔ The Grassmarket (➤ 47)

St Cecilia's Hall
✉ Cowgate
☎ 0131 650 2805
❓ Used for concerts by University of Edinburgh

The solid stone walls of Craigmillar Castle have defied the centuries

CRAIGMILLAR CASTLE ✪✪✪

You'll have to brave some of Edinburgh's poorer housing schemes to reach Craigmillar Castle, one of Scotland's most impressive medieval remains, standing in fields on the southeast side of the city. The L-plan tower dates from the mid to late 15th century and stands in a courtyard surrounded by curtain walls complete with massive corner towers. The castle was a favourite with Mary, Queen of Scots, and one of the two barrel-vaulted chambers is known as Queen Mary's Room. She fled to Craigmillar, 'wishing herself dead', after the murder of her secretary and favourite David Rizzio at Holyrood in 1566. Craigmillar later passed to the Gilmour family, who placed it in state care in 1946. Most children enjoy its empty spaces more than the packed precincts of Edinburgh's other, more famous castle.

➕ 79D3
✉ Craigmillar Castle Road
☎ 0131 661 4445
🕐 Apr–Sep, daily 9:30–6:30; Oct–Mar, Mon–Wed, Sat 9:30–4:30, Thu 9:30–1; Fri, Sun 2–4:30
🚌 2, 14, 42
🎫 Moderate

79D3

Cramond Ferry
✉ Cramond
☎ 0131 312 6653 (ferryman)
🕐 Sat–Thu; contact
   ferryman for times
🚌 40, 41

Dalmeny House
✉ Cramond
☎ 0131 331 1888
🕐 Park open Jul, Aug when
   house open; shore walk
   9–1, 2–7 (summer); 9–1,
   2–4 (winter); no access
   on Fri
🚌 40, 41

CRAMOND ⬤⬤

For a change from city sights, it's well worth making the short journey out to Cramond, a picturesque suburb on the shores of the Firth of Forth to the northwest of the city centre. Cramond was founded by the Romans, who established a harbour at the mouth of the River Almond in the 2nd century as a base for the soldiers constructing the Antonine Wall. Sections of the Roman fort, including a well-preserved bath-house, have been excavated, and an impressive Roman sculpture of a lion was found near the water's edge in 1997. Cramond has some attractive 16th-century houses, later, more elegant, villas, an old and famous inn and a lovely cruciform church, built in 1656. During the 18th century, Cramond's river position led to the establishment of four iron mills along the Almond; Scotland's first commercially produced steel came from here.

The weir on the River Almond Walkway

Today, you can follow the River Almond Walkway upriver or walk beside the shore of the Firth of Forth. Offshore lies Cramond Island, a grassy tidal island accessible at low tide if you don't mind scrambling over the slippery rocks and blocks of the causeway. Another alternative is to hail the **Cramond Ferry**, which has been running continuously since 1556, and cross the river to **Dalmeny House** (➤ 77), which has miles of parkland walks (accessible July and August) and a delightful shore walk to South Queensferry (accessible all year). On your way back into the centre, **Lauriston Castle** is worth a visit; this 16th-century tower house was extended in the 1820s and has some fine Edwardian interiors.

Lauriston Castle
✉ Cramond Road South,
   Davidson's Mains
☎ 0131 336 2060
🕐 Apr–Oct, Sat–Thu 11–1
   and 2–5; Nov–Mar, Sat,
   Sun 2–4. Note: guided
   tours only
🚌 40, 41
♿ Good
💷 Expensive (free access to
   grounds)
❓ Many indoor and outdoor
   events between spring
   and Christmas. Full
   details from Lauriston
   Castle

The Cramond Ferry has operated for centuries

DEAN VILLAGE ✪

Thomas Telford's Dean Bridge spans the steep gorge of the Water of Leith, which marks the northern limit of the New Town. Lying 32m below the bridge is Dean Village, a quiet and historic enclave with attractive old houses and easy access to the river. In medieval times the Dean was Edinburgh's milling centre, with 11 mills operating. Several 19th-century mill buildings still survive, now converted into flats – look out for Well Court, originally built as housing for workers in 1884. Baxter's Tolbooth is a 17th-century granary. Across the river Dean Cemetery overlooks the village. This 19th-century graveyard contains some of Edinburgh's finest funerary monuments, the best of them designed by William Playfair, the New Town architect, who himself is buried here.

➕ 28A3
✉ Dean Village
🍴 Restaurants and bars (£–£££)
🚌 19, 34, 40, 55
♿ Good
🔁 Stockbridge (▶ 68)

Fine old houses lining the Water of Leith in the Dean Village

DUDDINGSTON ✪

Crouched in the shadow of Arthur's Seat, the ancient settlement of Duddingston is one of Edinburgh's most attractive corners. Its pretty streets run down to Duddingston Loch, now part of a bird sanctuary and always thronged with geese and other wildfowl. This is the loch purportedly featured in the National Gallery's famous picture of the Reverend Walker skating (▶ 20). Duddingston Kirk is a 12th-century foundation, still retaining its Norman doorway and beautifully set in a verdant churchyard. Take time to wander around before heading for a drink in the Sheep's Heid Inn, dating from at least 1580 when it was patronised by James VI; it has the oldest skittle alley in Scotland.

➕ 79D3
✉ Duddingston
🍴 Sheep's Heid Inn (£–££)
🚌 4, 42, 43, 45
♿ Good
🔁 Holyrood Park (▶ 49)

DYNAMIC EARTH (▶ 17, TOP TEN)

41

Food & Drink

Scottish cuisine revels in fine local ingredients including wild salmon, beef and soft fruit such as raspberries; cakes and puddings are a speciality, and don't forget to sample some buttery shortbread and sweet Edinburgh Rock.

Succulent haggis with its traditional accompaniment, a glass of Scotch whisky

What to Eat in Edinburgh

No matter what you'd like to eat you'll probably find it in cosmopolitan Edinburgh, but seek out Scottish specialities, many of which you won't find south of the border.

Scottish Ingredients

Scotland has some of the best raw ingredients in the world, with land, river and sea contributing superb produce. Aberdeen Angus beef is renowned, game such as venison, grouse and pheasant is plentiful in season, and there's an abundance of the freshest of fish, shellfish and salmon, while Scotland's soft fruits have a special intensity of flavour. With such ingredients to hand, it seems ironic that the Scots diet was among Europe's unhealthiest, with the inhabitants revelling in oversalted and oversweetened dishes, and many Scots men proudly boasting they never ate vegetables. But things have changed radically in recent years and there's a renewed pride in local produce and traditional recipes.

Strawberries and champagne – the finest side of Scottish dining

Eating through the Day

Breakfast means porridge, the classic hot oatmeal dish, properly eaten with salt, but nicer with milk and sugar. Traditionally cured kippers are another favourite, or black or fruit pudding to accompany the egg and bacon. Oatcakes, soft 'morning rolls' and marmalade itself are all Scots originals. Lunch is the time for something light: a smoked-salmon sandwich, prawn salad or a bowl of good Scots soup. Scotch broth is famous, but try

cock-a-leekie, made with chicken, leeks and prunes, or cullen skink, a delicate fish and potato broth. Bridies, a pastry turnover stuffed with meat and onion, mutton pies, made with crisp hot-water pastry, and stovies, potato and onion, are traditional lunchtime favourites. Tea and baking are taken very seriously in Edinburgh, and you'll find excellent teashops and bakers churning out delectable scones, cakes and biscuits. Shortbread should be high on the list, and the sweet-toothed will love 'millionaires' shortbread' with its layers of soft toffee and chocolate. Dinner-time brings steaks, game and fish, plainly cooked or as the base for more sophisticated dishes. Haggis, the famous oatmeal, offal and onion dish traditionally simmered in a sheep's stomach, is delicious when properly made – a wee dram helps wash it down. Puddings are awesomely sweet; favourites include clootie dumpling, a heavy fruit pudding boiled in a cloth, Scots trifle, rich in sherry, raspberry jam and cream, or cranachan, made from toasted oatmeal folded into whipped sweetened cream and served with berries.

A choice of shapes and sizes for tartan-packed shortbread

From Whisky to Irn Bru

Tea is the liquid mainstay, with coffee gaining in popularity, and Edinburgh folk love fizzy sweet drinks, the entire nation's favourite being Irn Bru, famously 'brewed in Scotland from girders'. Scots beer differs from English; *heavy* is the nearest equivalent to English bitter and beers are graded by the shilling, a system indicating the potency – the higher the shilling, the stronger the beer. Look out for some of the beers from Edinburgh's small local breweries, or try *export* or lager. Whole volumes have been written about whisky. The choice lies between blended, a careful mix of grain and malt, and single malt – with literally hundreds to choose from. Try a few, find one you like and drink it neat or with water, the best way to appreciate its subtle flavour.

Just a modest selection of the hundreds of brands of whisky, on show in an Edinburgh speciality shop

Edinburgh Castle

✚ 28C2

✉ Edinburgh Castle, Castle Hill

☎ 0131 225 9846

◷ ➤ 18

🍴 Restaurant and café (£–££)

🚌 23, 27, 34, 35

♿ Few

💷 Very expensive

↔ Royal Mile (➤ 24–5)

Royal Scots Dragoon Guards Museum

☎ 0131 220 4387

◷ Apr–Oct, daily 9:30–5:30; Nov–Mar, daily 9:30–4:30

💷 Free

✚ 28B2

✉ Lothian Road and West Approach Road

🚌 11, 15, 24, 45

♿ Good

↔ Princes Street (➤ 59)

EDINBURGH CASTLE MUSEUMS ●●

Besides its ramparts, batteries, courtyards and fine buildings, **Edinburgh Castle** (➤ 18) also houses some interesting museums, mainly connected with Scotland's military past. Though not strictly a museum, the Scottish National War Memorial draws thousands of visitors to admire its austere splendours. Designed by Robert Lorimer in 1924, it first commemorated the more than 100,000 Scots who died in World War I. Near by is the Scottish United Services Museum, a military museum devoted to the uniforms and equipment of the armed forces in Scotland. Sections are devoted to the Royal Navy and Royal Air Force; there are no less than nine Victoria Crosses on display, together with a mass of paintings, photos and general military ephemera. **The Royal Scots Dragoon Guards**, Scotland's only cavalry regiment, have their own separate museum, with exhibits covering their 320-year history.

EDINBURGH EXCHANGE ●

It's well worth walking up the Lothian Road and along the West Approach Road to take a look at the £350-million-plus development known as the Edinburgh Exchange, the new financial district. The development plan was launched in 1988, after the construction of the palatial Sheraton Grand on what was then the rather run-down lower reaches of the Lothian Road. A clutch of buildings has gone up, centred around the Edinburgh International Conference Centre, opened in 1995 and designed by Terry Farrell. Building continues but the existing monuments to late 20th-century commerce, all soaring brick, stone and glass, are impressive enough. Worth noticing are the Standard Life building on the Lothian Road, with its fine gates and railings, and the impressive Scottish Widows building on Morrison Street.

The colourful figure of an ensign of the Royal Scots Dragoon Guards in the Edinburgh Castle Museum

A sweeping staircase leads upwards in the Hub Festival Centre

EDINBURGH'S FESTIVAL CENTRE – THE HUB ✪✪

More than 50 years after the first Edinburgh Festival and nearly 33 after moving into 'temporary' headquarters, in summer 1999 the Festival offices finally moved into a purpose-designed centre in the magnificently-converted Tolbooth at the top of the Royal Mile. The exterior, designed by Augustus Pugin for the Church of Scotland in the 1840s, remains unchanged, while inside you'll find some of Scotland's most exciting and innovative contemporary design. Sculptures, lighting, textiles and tiling make the mundane act of buying a ticket part of the Festival experience. The Hub is open year-round and provides a 'taste of the Festival' no matter when you come, with information and tickets on all the city's festivals throughout the year (➤ 116), a hall and library, restaurant, shop and other facilities.

➕ 28C2
✉ Castle Hill, Royal Mile
☎ 0131 473 2010; Café Hub 0131 473 2067
🕐 8AM–11PM
🍴 Café Hub (££)
🚌 23, 27, 34, 35
♿ Excellent
🎟 Free
↔ Camera Obscura (➤ 35); Edinburgh Castle (➤ 18); Scotch Whisky Heritage Centre (➤ 65)

EDINBURGH ZOO ✪✪✪

Spreading up the slopes of Corstorphine Hill, Edinburgh Zoo is the headquarters of the Royal Scottish Zoological Society, with a strong accent on conservation, captive breeding of endangered species and education. With over 1,000 animals from all over the world, plenty of hands-on opportunities and activities of all kinds, the Zoo is extremely child-friendly, and all kids will enjoy the chance to see rhinoceros, bears, giraffes, zebras, hippos and many more. A new lion enclosure has recently opened, there's the Magic Forest, devoted to small rainforest monkeys, and an evolutionary maze. The highlight for most visitors is the daily penguin parade at 2PM; the Zoo has a long tradition of successful breeding of four species of these charming birds, which you can see swimming underwater through the glass windows of their pool. Allow plenty of time for a visit, and be prepared to climb – Corstorphine Hill is steep.

➕ 79D3
✉ Murrayfield
☎ 0131 334 9171
🕐 Apr–Sep, daily 9–6; Oct, Nov, Mar daily 9–5:30; Jan–Feb daily 9–4:30
🍴 Cafeteria and kiosks (£–££)
🚌 2, 12, 31, 69
♿ Excellent; reduced admission for disabled visitors
🎟 Expensive
↔ Corstorphine (➤ 37); Murrayfield (➤ 57)
❓ Many special events aimed specifically at children

🔲 28C3
✉ George Street
🍴 Restaurants, bars and
cafés (£–£££)
🚌 12, 22, 33, 51
♿ Good
↔ Charlotte Square (➤ 36);
The Georgian House
(➤ below); Hanover
Street (➤ 48)

*This medicine chest
would have been a valued
travelling accoutrement
for the residents of the
Georgian House*

GEORGE STREET ⭐⭐

The central street of the three that form the grid of the first
stage of the 1766 New Town, George Street has escaped
the development that has wrecked the architecture of
Princes Street (➤ 59). This spacious thoroughfare,
designed by James Craig and named after George III, is
still liberally endowed with Georgian buildings, many of
them housing prestigious businesses and smart shops. St
Andrew's Church (1785), with its fine Corinthian portico,
stands near the east end; it was here, in 1843, that
dissenting ministers walked out of the General Assembly
to found the Free Church of Scotland. Further west, the
Assembly Rooms (1787) (➤ 33) are worth a visit, while
several of the opulent Victorian edifices which once
housed banks have been transformed into elegant and
lively wine bars, popular with Edinburgh's well-heeled
young professionals.

🔲 28B3
✉ 7 Charlotte Square
☎ 0131 226 3318
🕐 Apr–Oct, Mon–Sat 10–5,
Sun 2–5
🍴 Restaurants, bars and
cafés near by (£–£££)
🚌 12, 22, 33, 51
♿ None
💷 Expensive, but free to
National Trust and
National Trust for
Scotland members
↔ Charlotte Square (➤ 36);
George Street(➤ above);
Hanover Street (➤ 48)

THE GEORGIAN HOUSE ⭐⭐

The Georgian House, on the north side of Robert Adam's
Charlotte Square, offers a chance to see how Edinburgh's
monied classes lived in the grand houses of the New
Town. Reconstruction of the interior involved restoring the
original colour scheme, weaving fabrics for curtains and
coverings, and tracking down contemporary furniture,
rugs, paintings and fittings. You can see the ground-floor
dining room, laid up with Wedgwood and silver, and, in
true 18th-century style, a ground-floor bedroom, with a
dauntingly smart four-poster bed. The fashionably sparsely
furnished drawing room runs the full width of the house
upstairs, while the basement kitchen was the height of
convenience in Georgian times. It's crammed with utensils
and dominated by the huge range. Note the blue walls; it
was believed that blue kept the flies away.

*Above: a strikingly realistic brass scupture on the exterior wall at Gladstone's land
Left: a cosy panelled 17th-century bedchamber*

GLADSTONE'S LAND ✪✪

Gladstone's Land, a narrow, six-storey arcaded building and Edinburgh's finest surviving high-storey tenement, was purchased in 1617 by Thomas Gledstanes, a merchant and burgess. He was a prosperous man, with enough money both to buy and decorate this sizeable and prestigiously sited building. Gledstanes remodelled the house, using the arcaded ground floor as a shop, and letting all but one of the other floors, which he retained for his own use. Today, the ground-floor booths display 17th-century wares, while the first-floor rooms are furnished as the typical home of a wealthy citizen of that time. The main bedroom has a beautiful painted ceiling, decorated with fruit and flowers, and traces of the original frescoes which were painted on the walls.

THE GRASSMARKET ✪✪

Crouched below the Castle Rock, the long open space known as The Grassmarket is one of old Edinburgh's most attractive squares. With its cobbled pavement and groups of trees, it's often likened to a French *place*, and makes a pleasant place to pause for a little window-shopping and a drink at one of its bars or pubs. It was first chartered as a market in 1477 and served for more than 300 years as the city's main corn and live-stock market, besides being the site of the common gibbet. The Covenanters' Memorial commemorates the many citizens who were hanged here during the religious upheavals of the 17th century. The Grassmarket has been considerably smartened up in recent years, but still manages to retain something of the atmosphere Robert Burns must have felt when he wrote *Ae Fond Kiss* in the White Hart Inn.

✚ 29D2
✉ 477B Lawnmarket, Royal Mile
☎ 0131 226 5856
🕐 Apr–Oct, Mon–Sat 10–5, Sun 2–5
🚌 1, 23, 34, 42
♿ None
💷 Moderate, but free to National Trust and National Trust for Scotland members
↔ Camera Obscura (➤ 35); Edinburgh Castle (➤ 18); The Lawnmarket (➤ 51); Scotch Whisky Heritage Centre (➤ 65)

✚ 28C2
✉ The Grassmarket
🍴 Restaurants and cafés near by (£–££)
🚌 1, 28, 40
♿ Good
↔ Royal Mile (➤ 24–5); Victoria Street (➤ 70)

➕ 29D2
✉ 2 Greyfriars Place,
Candlemaker Row
☎ 0131 226 5429
🕐 Easter–Oct, Mon–Fri
10:30–4:30, Sat
10:30–2:30
🚌 1, 28, 40
♿ Few
💶 Free
↔ The Grassmarket (➤ 47);
Museum of Scotland
(➤ 19); Royal Mile
(➤ 24–5)

*Faithfulness personified –
the tiny statue of
Greyfriars Bobby*

GREYFRIARS KIRK ✪✪

Historic Greyfriars Kirk, standing on the site of a Franciscan friary, was built in 1620, a simple and peaceful church surrounded by a green kirkyard, the site of the signing of the National Covenant in 1638. Most visitors come here to see the statue of a small Skye terrier on a fountain opposite the churchyard gate. The statue commemorates Greyfriars Bobby, a loyal dog who kept watch here at his master's grave for 14 years until his own death in 1872.

➕ 28C4
✉ Hanover Street
🍽 Restaurants and cafés
near by (£–£££)
🚌 13, 20, 28, 80
♿ Good
↔ George Street (➤ 46);
New Town (➤ 21);
Queen Street (➤ 60)

HANOVER STREET ✪

For one of the best views to be had in the New Town, walk in either direction up and down the slopes of Hanover Street, the easternmost of the three streets crossing the grid pattern of the First New Town. To the south is the classical façade of the Royal Scottish Academy, with the Mound, Assembly Hall (➤ 33) and New College rising behind. To the north, the slopes drop away to give far views to the Firth of Forth and the Fife hills. The statue at the junction with George Street shows George IV, seemingly enjoying much the same vista.

➕ 29D2
✉ High Street
🍽 Restaurants and cafés
near by (£–£££)
🚌 1, 28, 40 45
♿ Good
↔ St Giles Cathedral
(➤ 64); Royal Mile
(➤ 24–5)

THE HEART OF MIDLOTHIAN ✪

Stand with your back to the entrance to St Giles Cathedral and move about twenty paces forward and slightly to your right. At your feet you'll see the outline of a heart laid out in cobblestones. This is the Heart of Midlothian, which marks the place of the old Tolbooth prison, where executions took place. If you really want to feel like a local, it's customary to spit on the spot.

Sharp eyes will easily pick out the Heart of Midlothian in the cobbles outside St Giles

HOLYROOD ABBEY ✪

You'll see the remains of the once-magnificent Holyrood Abbey, founded in 1128 by David I, on a visit to the Palace of Holyroodhouse (► 22). Legend tells that the king was thrown from his horse by a huge stag; while grappling with it he found a crucifix in his hands and later dreamt that he should found a monastery of the Holy Rood, or Cross, on the site. The present abbey was built for the Augustinians in the early 13th century, a cathedral-sized structure with a superb medieval façade. Burnt by the English in 1544, partially destroyed after the Reformation, the Abbey was the scene of Charles I's coronation. In 1588 it was sacked by the Edinburgh mob, who desecrated the royal tombs, and in 1768 much of the remaining fabric collapsed.

- ✚ 29F3
- ✉ The Palace of Holyroodhouse
- ☎ 0131 556 7371; recorded information 0131 556 1096
- 🕐 Apr–Oct, 9:30–6; Nov–Mar, 9:30–4:30. Closed Good Fri; 2wks early May; early Jun; late Jun to mid-Jul, 25–26 Dec. As the palace is a Royal residence, opening times may be subject to change at short notice – telephone to check.
- 🚌 1, 6
- ♿ Good
- 🎟 Expensive
- ↔ Arthur's Seat (► 16); Dynamic Earth (► 17); Holyrood Park (► below); Palace of Holyroodhouse (► 22); Royal Mile (► 24–5)

A surviving window gives a clue to the former glory of Holyrood Abbey

HOLYROOD PARK ✪✪✪

Once a royal hunting preserve, Holyrood Park, which includes Arthur's Seat (► 16), is unique among city parks. No other European city can boast a piece of wild countryside, complete with three lochs, dramatic cliffs and open moorland, within a stone's throw of its heart. When museums and sightseeing pall you can escape to the park to picnic, walk, feed the ducks and geese or simply relax and do nothing. Queen's Drive, built at the instigation of Prince Albert, runs right around the park and up towards Arthur's Seat; a pleasant drive, it's closed to all commercial vehicles. At its highest point you'll find Dunsapie Loch, another of Albert's inspirations. Don't miss St Margaret's Well, a medieval Gothic structure near Holyrood Palace where a clear spring wells from beneath sculpted vaulting.

- ✚ 29F2
- ✉ Holyrood Park
- ☎ 0131 556 3407
- 🕐 Open 24 hours, 365 days a year, but no vehicular access to Dunsapie Loch on Sun
- 🚌 1, 6, 36, 69. 85
- 🎟 Free
- ↔ Arthur's Seat (► 16) Duddingston (► 41); Dynamic Earth (► 17); Holyrood Abbey (► above); Palace of Holyroodhouse (► 22); Royal Mile (► 24–5)

29E3

142 Canongate, Royal Mile

0131 529 4143

Mon–Sat 10–5; during Edinburgh Festival, Sun 2–5

1, 6

Good

Free

Dynamic Earth (► 17); Holyrood Abbey (► 49); Holyrood Park (► 49); Palace of Holyroodhouse (► 22); The People's Story Museum (► 58)

Right: *this elegant gentleman, an exhibit in the Huntly House Museum, advertised the pleasures of tobacco* Opposite: *tall tenements, typical of Lawnmarket houses*

29E3

43–45 High Street, Royal Mile

0131 556 9579/2647

Mon–Sat 10–5; Sun during Edinburgh Festival 12–5

Café (£)

1, 6

Moderate

Museum of Childhood (► 57); Royal Mile (► 24); Tron Kirk (► 69)

Part of Netherbow Centre which also contains the Netherbow Theatre

HUNTLY HOUSE MUSEUM

The three tenements comprising the Huntly House Museum, a warren of passages, crooked stairs and oddly shaped rooms, are as fascinating as the collections they house, which tell the history of Edinburgh. The building dates from 1570, and was home to merchants, aristocrats and working people at different times in its history; you can see how they lived in the different room interiors scattered throughout. There's almost too much to see in one visit, with displays following Edinburgh's development from Roman times to the 19th century. The eclectic mix includes everything from silver to shop signs, but most visitors particularly enjoy the sight of Greyfriars Bobby's collar and bowl (► 48); while more serious-minded visitors shouldn't miss the 1638 National Covenant, signed by the Presbyterian leadership.

JOHN KNOX'S HOUSE ✪

Whether or not the key figure in Scotland's 16th-century Reformation actually died in the the building known as John Knox's House is open to debate, but the tradition was enough to prevent the destruction of this fine 1450 burgh house, all overhanging gables and picturesque windows. Today, it houses an exhibition on the complex subject of the Scottish Reformation, complete with an audio re-enactment of Knox's famous audience with Mary, Queen of Scots, when he condemned the Mass and her love of dancing. You can also learn about the house's other famous inhabitant, James Mossman, the goldsmith who made the Scottish Crown. He was probably responsible for the lovely carved frieze on the exterior that reads: LOVE. GOD. ABVFE. AL. AND. YI. NYCHTBOVR. AS. YI. SELF.

LADY STAIR'S HOUSE, THE WRITERS' MUSEUM ⭐

Duck through the narrow entrance of Lady Stair's Close and you'll emerge in an enclosed square, surrounded by high tenements. Robert Burns stayed here during his first visit to Edinburgh, an attractive thought for visitors to the Writer's Museum, which occupies a three-storey house on the Close. The mansion dates from 1622, and was built by a wealthy merchant whose daughter made it over to Lady Stair in 1719. (Lady Stair was the widow of the judge and Secretary of State John Dalrymple, 1st Earl of Stair, who was held largely responsible for the massacre of Glencoe.) The museum is devoted to Scotland's great trio – Robert Burns, Sir Walter Scott and Robert Louis Stevenson. There's much well-presented information on the lives and works of these writers in the form of memorabilia, documents and pictures, with sound guides to help you make the most of your visit. The museum also stages temporary exhibitions on different aspects of the writers' lives.

🕂 29D2

✉ Lady Stair's Close, The Lawnmarket, Royal Mile

☎ 0131 529 4901

🕐 Mon–Sat 10–5; Sun during Edinburgh Festival 2–5

🚌 1, 28, 34, 42

🎟 Free

↔ Camera Obscura (➤ 35); Edinburgh Castle (➤ 18); Edinburgh Castle Museums (➤ 44); Gladstone's Land (➤ 47); The Mound (➤ 56); Royal Mile (➤ 24–5); St Giles Cathedral (➤ 64)

❓ Changing temporary exhibitions on literary themes

THE LAWNMARKET ⭐

The Lawnmarket is the name given to the section of the Royal Mile below Castlehill and above the High Street. It is one of the oldest streets in Edinburgh, and originally formed the 12th-century nucleus of David I's burgh. Its name comes from the 'lawn' or cloth once sold here and by the late 17th century it was the smartest place to live. Running off The Lawnmarket are some of the Old Town's best examples of closes and vennels. There are no less than three entrances to James's Court, an 18th-century close, once the home of David Hume, the philosopher, and James Boswell, Dr Johnson's biographer. Milne's Court, to the west, went up in 1690, a planned development to try and ease the congestion in the Old Town. Look out too, for Brodie's Close, home to the notorious Deacon Brodie.

🕂 28C2

✉ The Lawnmarket

🍴 Restaurants, pubs and cafés near by (£–£££)

🚌 1, 28, 34, 42

♿ Good

↔ Camera Obscura (➤ 35); Edinburgh Castle ➤ 18); Edinburgh Castle Museums (➤ 44); Gladstone's Land (➤ 47); Lawnmarket (➤ 51); The Mound (➤ 56); Royal Mile (➤ 24–5); St Giles Cathedral (➤ 64)

In the Know

If you have only a short time to visit Edinburgh, or would like to get a real flavour of the city, here are some ideas:

10
Ways to be a Local

Don't jump when the 1 o'clock gun goes off – check your watch instead, all the locals do.

Don't denigrate Scotland, its institutions or its culture.

Buy a picnic and eat it in Princes Street Gardens with people from the offices near by.

Join the Sunday crowds at Ingliston Market, on the city's western outskirts.

Be sure to eat some local specialities – try the Atrium, Dubh Prais and the Witchery (► 92, 93, 97), or Maison Hector and Stac Polly (► 94, 96).

Buy a local newspaper for an insight into Edinburgh's preoccupations.

Spend an evening visiting a few of Edinburgh's pubs; they range from the cosmopolitan to the deeply traditional.

Take a Sunday stroll at Cramond, in Holyrood Park or the Botanic Garden.

Be friendly and forthcoming, Edinburgh people are warm-hearted and open and will go out of their way to help.

Have a game of golf at Braid Hills, Silverknowes or Craigmillar (► 114).

10
Good Places To Have Lunch

Byzantium (£)
Busy café offering vegetarian dishes, curries and excellent value buffet.
✉ 9 Victoria Street
☎ 0131 225 1768

Cornerstone Café (£)
A friendly self-service café right in the city centre, serving delicious home bakes all day. ✉ St John's Church, Lothian Road / Princes Street
☎ 0131 229 0212

Cramond Inn (££)
An English-style pub in the heart of old Cramond.
✉ Cramond Glebe Road
☎ 0131 336 2035

Daniel's Bistro (££)
This French-style bistro serves good food in a pretty conservatory setting. ✉ 88 Commercial Street, Leith ☎ 0131 553 5933

Elephant's Sufficiency
One of the Royal Mile's best bets for lunch. ✉ 170 High Street ☎ 0131 220 0666

Gustos (£)
Ideally situated on the Royal Mile, this cheery café serves food all day.
✉ 105 High Street ☎ 0131 558 3083

Kavio's (£)
A friendly Italian restaurant right on the waterfront serving excellent-value three-course lunches.
✉ 63 The Shore. Leith
☎ 0131 467 7746

Kay's Bar (£)
A cosy New Town pub serving straight-forward, good-value pub food. ✉ 39 Jamaica Street West
☎ 0131 225 1858

The Terrace Café (££)
Good light meals with a Scottish slant. ✉ Royal Botanic Garden, Inverleith Row ☎ 0131 552 0616

Valvona and Crolla (££)
Pizzas, pasta and genuine Italian dishes in a truly Italian atmosphere. ✉ 19 Elm Row ☎ 0131 556 6066

10
Top Activities

Walking – join a themed guided walk through historic Edinburgh.

Cycling – on city-centre cycle lanes or miles of off-road cycle paths; just remember it's a hilly city.

Swimming – pools range from state-of-the-art water complexes to splendid Victorian baths.

Golf – a good range of courses at different prices.

Skating – head for Murrayfield to enjoy ice-skating all year round.

A city-centre lunch spot with a friendly ambience

The scenic dry-ski slope at Hillend

Skiing – Europe's longest dry-ski slope lies just south of the city.

Tennis – you'll find tennis courts at city parks and private clubs.

Sports – keep fit or have a go at a choice of 60 sports at the Meadowbank Sports Centre (0131 661 5351).

Watersports – head for South Queensferry to try dinghy sailing or take a jet-boat ride round the Forth Bridges.

Helicopter flights – get a bird's-eye view of Edinburgh on a guided helicopter tour (☎ airport 0131 333 1000).

Top Edinburgh Souvenirs

Edinburgh Shortbread – track down Scotland's national biscuit from one of the specialist producers.

Edinburgh Rock – this super-sweet, multi-coloured rock differs from others in its range of flavours and its soft consistency.

Edinburgh Crystal ranges from delicate drinking ware to dazzling paperweights.

Books, prints and maps – a wide choice at city-centre bookshops and antiquarian specialists.

Tapes, CDs and videos of Edinburgh's top musicians, sights and events.

Splendid Statues

Allan Ramsay in West Princes Street Gardens; a marble statue of the 18th-century poet, carved from an 18-ton block by Sir John Steell, and erected in 1865.

David Livingstone in East Princes Street Gardens; a bronze statue of the 19th-century missionary and explorer, sculpted by Amelia Robertson Hill in 1876.

John Knox in Parliament Square; Knox is commemorated by a bronze statue standing against the wall of St Giles, designed by Pittendrigh MacGillivray in 1906.

The Duke of Wellington in Princes Street; a 12-ton bronze equestrian statue of the Iron Duke stands outside Register House; designed by Sir John Steell, it was one of the first successful prancing horses.

Charles II in Parliament Square; the oldest statue in Edinburgh and the oldest equestrian statue in Britain, designed by an unknown sculptor and dated 1685.

Great Views and Vistas

From the top of Arthur's Seat (➤ 16) – well worth the climb.

Spend time on the ramparts of Edinburgh Castle (➤ 18) looking at Princes Street and the New Town to the north.

From Calton Hill (➤ 35) – a sweeping vista towards Princes Street and the castle – even better from Nelson Monument (➤ 35).

Stand in the New Town (➤ 21) and experience the grandeur of Georgian town planning.

Drive out to South Queensferry to view the splendour of the two Forth bridges from below.

Climb the Scott Monument (➤ 26) for superb views along Princes Street, up the Mound and over towards the castle.

Stand in Melville Street and admire its spacious elegance dominated by the spires of St Mary's.

Don't miss the roof-terrace view at the Museum of Scotland (➤ 19).

Blackford Hill (➤ 34) gives wide views back towards the city centre, and the Firth of Forth and Fife hills.

• **Stand at the corner of The Lawnmarket** and the High Street for the best view of the Royal Mile (➤ 24–5).

Scottish shortbread is a favourite souvenir

🕀 79D3
✉ Leith
🍴 Wide range of
restaurants, cafés and
bars (£–£££)
🚌 1, 12, 16, 22, 35
♿ Good
↔ Royal Yacht *Britannia*
(▶ 63)

*New construction has
gone hand-in-hand with
restoration at Leith*

LEITH ★★

There's been less-than-friendly rivalry between Leith and Edinburgh over the centuries, dating from the days when the latter controlled all Leith's foreign trade – indeed, Leith was only amalgamated with the capital in 1920. Its history as a dock area dates from before the 14th century, though its existing docks and warehouses mainly went up in the 1800s. The docks are still working commercially and plans are afoot for the construction of a monster new terminal and shopping centre. This is one more sign of Leith's regeneration over recent years, making a trip down the Leith Walk, which links it to the centre, a good option for a change of pace.

Head first for the Shore, a lovingly restored area by the Water of Leith, with desirable flats and many excellent bars and restaurants. Nearby warehouses have also been converted to up-market accommodation; you can see these on Commercial Street, which gives access to the quay where the Royal Yacht *Britannia* (▶ 63) is moored. The impressive post-modern building housing the Scottish Office also draws the eye. East of the Shore one or two older buildings have survived near the Kirkgate, the old town centre, now wrecked by a disastrous shopping arcade and high-rise flats. Leith Links lies further east again, a pleasant green space much favoured by local dogs. The Links claims to be one of the earliest homes of golf; the ground was in use for golf in 1593 and it was here that the first set of rules was formulated.

THE MEADOWS ✪

The open grassy space known as the Meadows, criss-crossed with paths and studded with trees, is popular with students from the university, doctors and nurses from the nearby Royal Infirmary and families from the surrounding residential streets. It's a good place to relax or let your children run about, and there's a playground with slides and swings. The whole area was once covered by the Burgh Loch, which supplied Edinburgh's water. Piped water arrived in 1676, the loch was drained in the 18th century and the Meadows became a public park in 1860. Twenty-six years later the grand International Exhibition of Industry was held here; the Whalebone Arch is a relic of this. Enjoy the Meadows by day, but its paths are better avoided if you're alone at night.

✚ 29D1
⊠ The Meadows
♿ Good
🚌 11, 15, 16 23
↔ University of Edinburgh
(► 69)

MERCAT CROSS ✪

Spare a few moments as you walk down the Royal Mile to admire the Mercat Cross outside St Giles, one of the most evocative symbols of Edinburgh. Today's version dates from the 1880s and is modelled on the 17th-century cross; it was restored in 1970 and again in 1990, when the eight medallions showing the arms of Britain, Scotland, England and Ireland and another four connected with Edinburgh were gilded. In medieval times the Mercat Cross was the focus for trade, and there's probably been a cross on this site since the 12th century. Public festivities took place here, royal proclamations were read, and executions performed. In 1513 the troops set out from here on the fateful march to defeat at the Battle of Flodden.

✚ 29D2
⊠ High Street
♿ Good
🚌 1, 28, 34, 42
↔ Parliament House (► 58);
Parliament Square
(► 58); St Giles Cathedral
(► 64)

Right and above: *medallions on the Mercat Cross alluding both to Great Britain and the City of Edinburgh*

79D3
Morningside
Restaurants, pubs and
cafés (£–£££)
5, 11, 27, 45
Good
Blackford Hill (➤ 34)

MORNINGSIDE

Tucked away in the quiet, leafy streets of Morningside on the southwest side of Edinburgh are solid Victorian villas still housing the prosperous citizens of Edinburgh's middle classes. Morningside, its respectability the butt of countless jokes, is one of several suburbs developed in the 19th century for the growing bourgeoisie, who wanted to live neither in the cold grandeur of the New Town nor the increasing squalor of the Old. The area is approached via 'Holy Corner', the affectionate local name for a crossroads surrounded by no less than four churches. Morningside, with its good shops, services and local amenities, has all a suburb could wish for; a stroll round here provides that insight into local life which is often so hard to find in major cities.

28C3
The Mound
2, 10, 20 45
Very good
Princes Street (➤ 59);
Princes Street Gardens
(➤ 59); National Gallery
of Scotland (➤ 20); Royal
Scottish Academy (➤ 61)

*The slopes of The Mound
and the towers of the
Assembly Hall behind*

THE MOUND

Until the 1760s the site now occupied by Princes Street Gardens was filled with an unlovely lake known as the Nor' Loch, created as a northern defence for the castle in 1460. In 1763 it was partially drained for the construction of the North Bridge, to allow access to the planned New Town. To the west the marshy ground was gradually bridged by the mounds of earth from the building works to the north; by 1784 it was a rough causeway for carriages and was completed by 1830. An estimated two million cartloads of dumped earth went into its construction – a veritable mound. Its two landmarks are the Royal Scottish Academy (➤ 61) and the National Gallery of Scotland (➤ 20).

MURRAYFIELD ✪✪

The western suburb of Murrayfield, all terraces and villas, was developed around 18th-century Murrayfield House in the 1860s. It's a comfortable, well-to-do area with good local amenities and easy access both to the city centre and the green slopes of Corstorphine Hill (➤ 37). Twice a year Murrayfield comes into its own as crowds pour out from town to Murrayfield Stadium, the home of Scotland's international rugby union team, where home games are played during what is now (2000) the Six Nations championship. The stadium, vastly extended and modernised over the years, was built in 1925 by the then Scottish Football Union. The first game was played in March that year, when Scotland beat England 14–11.

➕ 28A2
✉ Murrayfield
☎ Murrayfield Stadium 0131 346 5000
🚌 2, 26, 31, 63
♿ Good
↔ Corstorphine (➤ 37); Edinburgh Zoo (➤ 45)

MUSEUM OF CHILDHOOD ✪✪✪

The Museum of Childhood is a delight, its five galleries crammed with everything from trainsets and tiddlywinks to teddies and tricycles. It started life in 1955 as the brainchild of town councillor Patrick Murray, who, right from the start, set his own distinctive mark on the vast range of exhibits – many of the quirky and informative labels were written by him. Apart from the huge collection of toys from all over the world, many of them very old indeed, there are sections devoted to children's clothes, books, education, food and medicine. You can watch re-runs of old cartoons, listen to playground songs and children chanting multiplication tables and admire some truly palatial dolls' houses. The galleries constantly echo with the cry 'I remember that' as grannies, mums and kids rediscover the joys and pains of childhood.

➕ 29E3
✉ 42 High Street, Royal Mile
☎ 0131 529 4142
🕐 Mon–Sat 10–5; Sun during Edinburgh Festival 2–5
🚌 1, 6, 27, 45
♿ Very good
🆓 Free
↔ Gladstone's Land (➤ 47); The Lawnmarket (➤ 51); The Mound (➤ 56); Royal Mile (➤ 24–5); St Giles Cathedral (➤ 64)

MUSEUM OF SCOTLAND (➤ 19, TOP TEN)

NATIONAL GALLERY OF SCOTLAND (➤ 20, TOP TEN)

THE NEW TOWN (➤ 21, TOP TEN)

PALACE OF HOLYROODHOUSE (➤ 22, TOP TEN)

Left: *a sign above the entrance at the Museum of Childhood*

57

PARLIAMENT HOUSE

From 1639 until the Treaty of Union in 1707 the Scots Parliament met in Parliament House, a superb 17th-century Scottish Renaissance building just behind St Giles Cathedral. The long and lofty main chamber, Parliament Hall, was home to the 'Three Estates' – no distinction was made in Scotland between clergy, nobility and burgesses. The Scottish MPs processed from here in July 1999 before the opening of the new Scottish Parliament (➤ 66). The hall has a magnificent hammerbeam roof and a fine 19th-century stained-glass window. The building is now occupied by law courts and advocates' chambers, and there's an interesting display on its history and present use.

> ### DID YOU KNOW?
>
> Scotland has its own legal system, distinct from that used in England. Scots Law was preserved by the 1707 Treaty of Union and is based largely on Roman and Canon Law to which English Common Law methods are applied. It has been instrumental in preserving the strong Scottish sense of identity.

PARLIAMENT SQUARE

Parliament Square lies behind St Giles Cathedral, an open space surrounded by the 19th-century colonnades masking Parliament House; they were designed by Robert Reid and built between 1803 and 1830. The equestrian statue of Charles II excited much comment when it went up in 1685, Roman triumphal dress being less than familiar to the locals. You'll see lawyers hurrying through the square on their way to the Court of Session and the High Court of Justice.

THE PEOPLE'S STORY MUSEUM

For an insight into Edinburgh's social history pause on your way down the Royal Mile to visit The People's Story, a fascinating museum crammed with the minutiae of everyday life. There's a wealth of artefacts and informative displays on everything from local bakers and brewers to Edinburgh tea rooms and pubs. The reconstructions of rooms are particularly interesting, and provide a graphic illustration of the extent of Edinburgh's housing problems right into the 20th century.

One of the museum's fascinating interiors

29D2
Parliament Square
Mon–Fri 9–5
1, 28, 34, 42
Few
Free
Mercat Cross (➤ 55); Parliament Square (➤ below); Royal Mile (➤ 25); St Giles Cathedral (➤ 64)

29D2
Parliament Square
Mon–Fri 9–5
1, 28, 34, 42
Good
Mercat Cross (➤ 55); Parliament House (➤ 59); Royal Mile (➤ 24–5); St Giles' Cathedral (➤ 65)

29E3
Canongate Tolbooth, 163 Canongate, Royal Mile
0131 529 4057
Mon–Sat 10–5; Sun during Edinburgh Festival 2–5
1, 6
Good
Free
Dynamic Earth (➤ 17); Palace of Holyroodhouse (➤ 22)

PRINCES STREET ✪✪✪

Its situation alone makes Princes Street one of Europe's great thoroughfares, a straight and stately division between the Old Town and the New, with views south across Princes Street Gardens to the fabulous silhouette of the castle and Royal Mile. Lined with department and high street stores, Princes Street is where Edinburgh people come to shop, and its pavements are thronged throughout the day. Built from 1769, it was named after George III's two sons, the monarch having rejected the name St Giles Street, after Edinburgh's patron saint. Princes Street once presented the elegant and harmonious face of restrained Georgian architecture, but began to deteriorate in the 19th century and has gone downhill ever since, as dignified buildings have been torn down and replaced with some of the worst excrescences of the mid to late 20th century.

➕ 28B3
✉ Princes Street
🍴 Wide range of cafés, bars and restaurants (£–££)
🚌 2, 10, 15, 26, 33, 45
♿ Very good
🔄 National Gallery of Scotland (➤ 20); New Town (➤ 21); Royal Scottish Academy (➤ 61); Scott Monument (➤ 26)

The world's oldest independent department store is an Edinburgh institution

PRINCES STREET GARDENS ✪✪✪

The green oasis of Princes Street Gardens occupies the site of the old Nor' Loch (➤ 56), drained during the construction of the New Town. The 8ha West Gardens, laid out in 1816–20 for the Princes Street inhabitants, are separated from the 3ha East Garden by the bulk of the Royal Scottish Academy (➤ 61); both gardens became a much-loved public park in 1876. They are laid out conventionally and attractively with specimen trees, sweeping lawns and riotously bright planting. Children will love the Floral Clock in the West Garden, planted every year on a different theme; watch out for the cuckoo when the hour strikes. The gardens are edged with statues, which include the explorer David Livingstone, and James Young Simpson, the pioneer of the safe use of chloroform.

➕ 28C3
✉ Princes Street
🍴 Snack bars and kiosks in gardens (£)
🚌 2, 10, 15, 26, 33, 45
♿ Very good
🔄 National Gallery of Scotland (➤ 20); New Town (➤ 21); Royal Scottish Academy (➤ 61); Scott Monument (➤ 26)

28C4

✉ Queen Street

🍴 Restaurants and cafés near by

🚌 13, 20, 28, 37

♿ Good

↔ George Street (➤ 46); Hanover Street (➤ 48); New Town (➤ 21); Scottish National Portrait Gallery (➤ 66)

A carved relief in the wall above the street sign at Queen Street

29D3

✉ Scottish Record Office, 2 Princes Street

☎ 0131 535 1314

🕐 Mon–Fri 9–4:30

🚌 2, 10, 15, 26, 33, 45

♿ Good

🎟 Free

↔ Princes Street (➤ 59); Royal High School (➤ below); Scott Monument (➤ 26)

29E3

✉ Regent Road

🚌 2, 5, 22, 34

↔ Princes Street (➤ 59); Register House (➤ above)

QUEEN STREET ✪✪

Queen Street runs parallel with Princes Street (➤ 59) and George Street (➤ 46), a long stretch of fine Georgian architecture that is largely untouched by modern development. Queen Street was built between 1769 and 1792 and named after Queen Charlotte, wife of George III. Most of its buildings now house offices, but the fine views towards the Firth of Forth remain unchanged, as do the private gardens running

along the whole of the north side. James Young Simpson, the pioneer of anaesthesia, conducted his experiments on himself in number 52.

REGISTER HOUSE ✪

Specifically designed by Robert Adam in 1774 to house the national archives, Register House still fulfils that purpose today. The domed rectangular building, considered to be Edinburgh's finest neo-classical structure, contains a plethora of documents of national importance. If you want to trace Scottish forebears, start here; the records are open to everyone, the staff are helpful and you can pick up a copy of *Tracing Scottish Local History* to help you find your way around. Further registers are held in West Register House in Charlotte Square.

ROYAL BOTANIC GARDEN (➤ 23, TOP TEN)

ROYAL HIGH SCHOOL ✪

Many visitors wonder about the monumental building, visible from many parts of the city, that once housed the Royal High School. This huge Greek Doric edifice was designed by Thomas Hamilton in 1829 – he based his plan on the Temple of Theseus in Athens. In 1976 the building was converted into a debating chamber destined to house the new Scottish Parliament. That year the referendum turned down devolution; when it came in 1999, the government rejected the school and chose a site at Holyrood for the new parliament building (➤ 66).

ROYAL MILE (➤ 24–5, TOP TEN)

ROYAL SCOTTISH ACADEMY ✪

This lovely classical building, designed by William Playfair in 1822, is a fitting home for Scotland's Royal Academy, which moved here permanently in 1910. The Academy, founded in 1826, is based loosely on London's Royal Academy, and has both Academicians and Associates. It is at the forefront of art promotion in Scotland and to this end holds two major exhibitions annually; the Students Art Exhibition and the Annual Exhibition. The Academy also lets the building to other arts organisations, such as the Royal Scottish Society of Painters in Watercolour and the Society of Scottish Artists, who stage their shows in the spacious galleries. It is also an important Festival exhibition venue, when its steps are thronged with Festival-goers enjoying the street theatre in the square outside.

🕇 28C3
⊠ The Mound
☎ 0131 225 6671
🕐 Mon–Sat 10–5; Sun 2–5 (6PM during Festival)
🚌 2, 10, 15, 26, 33, 45
♿ Very good
💷 Varies according to exhibition
↔ Princes Street (➤ 59); The Mound (➤ 56); National Gallery of Scotland (➤ 20)

ROYAL SCOTTISH OBSERVATORY ✪

The Royal Scottish Observatory moved from Calton Hill (➤ 35) in 1895 when light pollution was starting to interfere with observations from the city-centre site. This is still very much a working observatory, charged with the task of collating material for astronomers world-wide from the UK's telescopes here and overseas, and housing sophisticated equipment. There's an excellent visitor centre, which will keep even those theoretically uninterested in astronomy fascinated for hours, and children will enjoy the multimedia gallery, which has plenty of hands-on activities and interactive exhibits. The roof terrace has far-reaching views north to the city centre; if you're in Edinburgh during the winter, there are weekly Friday-evening viewing sessions at the observatory.

🕇 28C1
⊠ Blackford Hill
☎ 0131 668 8405
🕐 Mon–Sat 10–5, Sun 12–5
🚌 24, 38, 41
♿ Few
💷 Moderate
↔ Blackford Hill (➤ 34); Braid Hills (➤ 34)

The solid Victorian bulk of the Royal Observatory houses up-to-date equipment

New Town and Princes Street

Distance
4km/2.5 miles

Time
1½ hours walking; 4 hours
with stops for visits

Start/end point
Charlotte Square
 28B3
2, 13, 24, 36

*Walk down North Charlotte Street and cross
Queen Street to continue down Forres Street to
Moray Place. Turn right and exit into
Darnaway Street and along to Heriot Row.
Continue along Heriot Row and cross the top of
Howe Street to look at No 17 Heriot Row.*

As you walk along Heriot Row, Queen Street Gardens are
on your right; these were part
of the New Town's original plan
to give householders access to
green space. Number 17 Heriot
Row was the childhood home
of Robert Louis Stevenson;
look out for the plaque beside
the front door.

The Home of
ROBERT LOUIS STEVENSON
1857 – 1880

*Retrace your steps to turn
right down Howe Street
then right again on to Northumberland
Street. Where it meets Dundas Street turn right
uphill, crossing Heriot Row and Queen Street to
continue uphill on Hanover Street. Take the
first right into Thistle Street and walk along to
Frederick Street.*

Lunch
The Laigh Bakehouse (£)
117A Hanover Street
0131 225 1552

Thistle Street is one of the New Town's hidden and
seductive shopping streets, where you'll find antique
jewellers, up-market clothes shops and attractive cafés.

*Turn left uphill, cross George Street and
continue down to Princes Street. Turn left and
cross the road.*

You could take this opportunity to climb the Scott
Monument (► 26) or visit the Royal Scottish Academy
(► 61) or the National Gallery of Scotland (► 20), which
stands just behind it.

*With your back to the castle turn left along
Princes Street or walk through Princes Street
Gardens (► 59). At the end of the gardens,
cross Princes Street and go straight ahead up
South Charlotte Street.*

The dining room of the Royal Yacht Britannia, *with the table laid as it would have been for state banquets on board*

THE ROYAL YACHT *BRITANNIA* ✪✪✪

In 1953 the ocean-going Royal Yacht *Britannia* was launched on Clydebank, built to the highest specifications of the day. She remained in service for over 40 years, travelling more than a million miles to every corner of the world on voyages that included 968 official and state visits, family holidays and royal honeymoons. For the Queen and her family *Britannia* was 'home', a place to work, entertain and relax. Now fully restored and moored at Leith, *Britannia* still contains the fittings, furnishings, paintings and photographs from her working days. Tours start in the visitor centre, where exhibits and film tell the yacht's story. From here visitors follow a route round the yacht with an audio handset, whose soundtrack explains the different areas on show. These include the bridge, the Queen's bedroom and sitting room, the splendid dining room, the decks and the engine room.

ST ANDREW SQUARE ✪

Edinburgh's financial heart, St Andrew Square, lies at the east end of George Street, and was designed to act as the architectural counterbalance to Charlotte Square at the west end. Its design, dating from 1767, is not as instantly pleasing, but many of its features are older than they look. The grandiose mansion on the east side, built in 1772 for Sir Laurence Dundas, now houses the headquarters of the Royal Bank of Scotland; another Dundas, Henry, 1st Earl of Melville, surveys much of the New Town from the top of the 41m column in the centre of the square. Many of Edinburgh's trendier bars lie in or near the square.

🚩 79D3
✉ Ocean Drive, Leith
☎ 0131 555 5566
🕐 Apr–Oct, 10:30–6 (last tour 4:30); Nov–Mar, 10:30–4:30 (last tour 3:50)
🍴 Café in visitor centre (£–££)
🚌 10, 16, 22, 88 or X50 direct from Waverley Bridge
♿ Excellent
💷 Very expensive
↔ Leith (▶ 54)
❓ Booking strongly advised

🚩 29D4
✉ St Andrew Square
🍴 Range of restaurants, bars and cafés (£–£££)
🚌 2, 10, 28, 45
♿ Good

63

29D2

✉ Parliament Square

☎ 0131 225 9442

🕐 Mon–Sat 9–5 (later in summer), Sun 1–5

🚌 1, 27, 34, 40

♿ Very good

💷 Free – donation for entrance to Thistle Chapel

↔ Parliament House (➤ 64)

ST GILES CATHEDRAL ●●

St Giles Cathedral, the High Kirk of Edinburgh, dark and atmospheric, dates mainly from the 14th and 15th centuries. The oldest parts of the church are the four massive columns surrounding the Holy Table in the crossing; these support the central lantern, with its flying buttresses and spire, raised in 1500. The original cruciform church was widened by the construction of extra chapels; the choir, which dates to 1419, is among the finest pieces of medieval architecure in Scotland. Another highlight is the Thistle Chapel, an exquisite Gothic Revival masterpiece designed by Robert Lorimer in 1909 for the knights of the chivalric Order of the Thistle. St Giles was John Knox's church; here he preached until his death in 1572, struggling to establish Presbyterianism as Scotland's faith during the reign of Mary, Queen of Scots. Here too, the religious disturbances of 1637 began when the new Prayer Book, similar to the English Prayer Book, was introduced; this led to the signing of the National Covenant abolishing Episcopacy.

The central aisle and graceful arches of St Mary's

28A2

✉ Palmerston Place

☎ 0131 225 6293

🕐 Mon–Fri 7:30AM–6PM; Sat, Sun 7:30AM–5PM (summer months till 9PM)

🚌 2, 22, 30, 43

♿ Very good

💷 Free

↔ Charlotte Square (➤ 36)

❓ Regular programme of organ recitals and concerts; choral evensong during term-time. Phone the cathedral for further information.

ST MARY'S EPISCOPAL CATHEDRAL ●

In 1870, the Misses Barbara and Mary Coates, devoted Episcopalians, left a legacy in the shape of land and money for the building of a cathedral in the West End of Edinburgh. St Mary's, with the sisters' 17th-century mansion still in its shadow, is the result, a soaring Victorian Gothic creation which dominates this part of the city. It was designed by Sir George Gilbert Scott and built between 1874 and 1879, a cruciform church whose central tower rises to 84m – the full effect is best seen from Melville Street. The twin western towers were added in 1917, and are affectionately known as Barbara and Mary, in memory of the cathedral's donors. The interior combines architectural sobriety with a pious cosiness; look out for the glowing murals by Phoebe Anna Traquair, a leading figure in the Arts and Crafts movement.

SCOTCH WHISKY HERITAGE CENTRE ✪✪✪

Scotland's national drink is the theme of this entertaining and informative visitor centre, which attracts visitors from all over the world. If you want to learn about the history, manufacture and blending of whisky, head here – there's even a free dram to round off your visit. A film first gives a quick tour round a distillery; this is followed by a short talk on the different whisky regions and the effect of local conditions on the taste and 'nose' of the spirit, with a chance to have a sniff yourself. Next, a genie emerges from a bottle to tell you about blending before directing you to a journey through time – a ride in a barrel-car through 300 years of whisky history, complete with appropriate scents and sounds.

🬂 28C2
✉ 354 Castlehill, Royal Mile
☎ 0131 220 0441
🕔 Daily 10–5:30 (hours may be extended in summer – telephone to check)
🍴 Restaurant and bar (££)
🚌 1, 6, 27, 45
♿ Excellent
💷 Expensive
♿ Edinburgh Castle (➤ 18); Royal Mile (➤ 24–5)
❓ Tour includes free dram of whisky; over 200 varieties available for sale in shop

SCOTT MONUMENT (➤ 26, TOP TEN)

THE SCOTTISH NATIONAL GALLERY OF MODERN ART AND THE DEAN GALLERY ✪✪

An afternoon in Edinburgh's superbly designed and exciting modern art galleries makes a fascinating and stimulating contrast to medieval and Georgian Edinburgh. In 1999 Edinburgh's permanent exhibition space for modern art doubled with the opening of the Dean Gallery. The two galleries lie on either side of Belford Road, the Gallery of Modern Art housed in a 19th-century neo-classical ex-school, the Dean in a slightly earlier ex-hospital. The Gallery of Modern Art has a fine collection of international and Scottish 20th-century art, with examples of modern art movements such as Expressionism, Fauvism, and Surrealism. Look out for Francis Bacon and Jackson Pollock. Across the road, the Dean contains Edinburgh's renowned Dada and Surrealist collection, as well as many works by Eduardo Paolozzi, the Scottish sculptor whose work you may also have seen in the Museum of Scotland (➤ 19).

🬂 28A3
✉ Belford Road
☎ 0131 624 6200
🕔 Mon–Sat 10–5, Sun 2–5 (till 6PM during Festival).
🍴 Café in Gallery of Modern Art (£–££)
🚌 13
♿ Very good
💷 Free
❓ Charges for special exhibitions

True or false? – see if you can spot these figures in the Gallery of Modern Art

🔲 29D4
✉ 1 Queen Street
☎ 0131 624 6200
🕐 Mon–Sat 10–5, Sun 2–5
(till 6PM during Festival)
🍴 Café (£–££)
🚌 13, 27, 35, 80
♿ Very good
👐 Free
↔ Queen Street (➤ 60)
❓ Charges for special
exhibitions

🔲 29F3
✉ Lawnmarket (Debating
Chamber); George IV
Bridge (Parliament
headquarters); George IV
Bridge (visitor centre)
☎ 0845 278 1999/0131 348
5000
🕐 Visitor centre: Mon–Fri
9:30–5; Sat Jul–Aug
9:30–1, 2–5. Closed 24
Dec–4 Jan. Debating
Chamber: open during
parliamentary sessions
(Wed AM; Thu all day)
🚌 1, 6, 27, 45
♿ Visitor centre excellent;
Debating Chamber
excellent
👐 Free
↔ The Lawnmarket (➤ 51);
Royal Mile (➤ 24–5)

*Tiers of seats for
members in the
temporary home of the
Scottish Parliament*

SCOTTISH NATIONAL PORTRAIT GALLERY

The imposing red sandstone bulk of the Scottish National Portrait Gallery looms over the east end of Queen Street. Built in the 1880s, it's worth a visit for the interior alone, with its wonderful arcaded entrance hall glittering with lustrous murals. The entire collection is devoted to the Scots, though not all the portraits are *by* Scots. You can trace the flow of Scottish history and achievement through this diverse collection, though most people head straight for Mary, Queen of Scots, Nasmyth's portrait of Robert Burns and Raeburn's *Sir Walter Scott*. Modern Scots to look out for include Jean Muir, the fashion designer, Sean Connery, alias James Bond, and Irvine Welsh, the author of *Trainspotting*.

THE SCOTTISH PARLIAMENT ✪✪

Nearly 300 years after its last session, the Scottish Parliament opened once more in July 1999. Until 2002, when it moves to its new home at Holyrood, Parliament is housed in a clutch of buildings around the Royal Mile. Debating takes place in the Assembly Hall (➤ 33) of the Church of Scotland, while the headquarters and committee chambers are lodged a little further down the hill. The

committee chamber building also houses the visitor centre, where you can learn all about Scottish devolution and the working of Parliament through displays and interactive systems, with friendly staff on hand to answer questions. There's also a detailed model of the new Parliament Building. If you want to attend a debate, you can book in advance, or take a chance and go to the public entrance in Milne's Court.

DID YOU KNOW?

Until the new parliament building at Holyrood opens in 2002 the only refreshments on offer to Scottish Members of Parliament are strictly non-alcoholic. As the present parliament chamber belongs to the Church of Scotland their non-tolerance of the demon drink is being respected and MPs are making do with tea and biscuits.

The Water of Leith

From Queensferry Street turn left steeply down Bell's Brae to join the Water of Leith Walkway in Dean Village.

This is a good opportunity to explore the village (➤ 41).

Walk downstream, under the soaring Dean Bridge to reach St Bernard's Well.

This elegant columned temple, with its statue of the Roman goddess Hygeia, marks the sulphurous mineral springs of St Bernard's Well, discovered by three schoolboys in the 1760s. It quickly became popular as a healing centre. The wellhouse was designed by Alexander Nasmyth in 1789.

Turn left and cross the river, then right down Dean Terrace to the centre of Stockbridge (➤ 68). Cross Deanhaugh Street and rejoin the riverside path. Continue to Bridge Place, then cross the road and turn right up Arboretum Avenue. As the river curves, turn right along Rocheid Path.

You are now opposite the rows of streets known as The Colonies (➤ 37).

Follow the path down Inverleith Terrace Lane and turn left into Inverleith Row. After 183m turn left to enter the Royal Botanic Garden (➤ 23, Top Ten) and walk through by whichever route you like to Arboretum Place on the west side of the gardens. Cross the road and walk straight through Inverleith Park to Fettes Avenue.

The soaring and ornate building in front of you is Fettes College, the school where Tony Blair was educated.

Turn left down Fettes Avenue and continue, then turn left at the junction with Comely Bank Road, which becomes Raeburn Place.

Distance
4.8km (3 miles)

Time
1½ hours walking; 2–2½ with visit to Royal Botanic Garden

Start Point
Queensferry Street
🚶 28A3
🚌 19, 34, 40, 55

End Point
Raeburn Place
🚶 Off map
🚌 19, 20, 28, 34

Lunch
River Café (£)
✉ 36 Deanhaugh Street
☎ 0131 332 3322

A waterside café in Stockbridge makes a good place to pause

28B4
Stockbridge
19, 20, 28, 34
Good
The Colonies (➤ 37);
Royal Botanic Garden
(➤ 23); Water of Leith
(➤ 70)

STOCKBRIDGE

Situated at the bottom of the slopes of the New Town, the lively residential district of Stockbridge was once a milling and tanning village lying alongside the Water of Leith (➤ 70) and was the access point for livestock entering the city. In 1786 the present stone bridge was built and over the next 100 years Stockbridge gradually merged with Edinburgh as the tenement buildings, trim terraces and genteel villas went up. By the 1970s the area was crumbling, ripe for students, artists and the first alternative life-stylers, who moved in attracted by the low rents. In their wake came shops and restaurants, gentrification followed and Stockbridge once more became a desirable place to live. It's an alluring mélange of smart and cosy, where traditional foodshops rub shoulders with trendy bars and designer outlets. Make for St Stephen's Street to get a lingering taste of 1970s Stockbridge, before heading along the water's edge footpath to explore the Water of Leith (➤ 67, 70).

79D3
Swanston
4, 27, 32, 52 followed by walk
Few

These picturesque Swanston cottages seem a thousand miles from the bustling city centre

SWANSTON

Driving is the simplest way to get to Swanston, perhaps the prettiest of all Edinburgh's 'villages' and barely part of the city at all. Separated from the urban sprawl by the southern bypass and lying on the slopes of the Pentlands, the centre of this conservation village has changed little since the 19th century. A group of thatched cottages clusters round the village green together with the original 18th-century farmhouse and old school. Swanston is best known for its links with Robert Louis Stevenson (➤ 14); he came to spend the summers here annually with his family and nurse from 1867 to 1880.

TALBOT RICE ART GALLERY ✪

The Talbot Rice Art Gallery, a huge and airy balconied building that opened in 1975, lies just off the Old Quad of the University of Edinburgh. It houses the Torrie Collection, a pleasing small collection of Dutch and Italian Old Masters. The gallery is probably better known for its changing exhibitions, which run all year round, with shows by established Scottish and other artists.

29D2
Old College, South Bridge
0131 650 2210
Tue–Sat 10–5; daily during Festival
7, 14, 28, 45
Good
Free, but charges for some exhibitions
Museum of Scotland (➤ 19); University of Edinburgh (➤ below)
Temporary exhibitions throughout the year

The Tron Kirk is now owned by the city council, and houses an exhibition on Old Town history

THE TRON KIRK ✪✪

Christ's Kirk at the Tron, a fine Palladian-Gothic church built between 1637 and 1663, got its name from the salt-tron, a public weighbeam, which stood outside. In 1785, the south aisle was demolished to make room for the bridges linking the Old and New Towns. Closed for worship since 1952, the Tron now houses the Old Town Information Centre, which will fill you in on what to do and where to go in and around the Royal Mile. It also has excellent displays on Old Town history. You can see the remains of Marlin's Wynd inside the Tron; this 16th-century street was destroyed to make room for the church, and only excavated in the 1970s.

29D3
High Street, Royal Mile
0131 225 8818
Easter–Jun and Sep, daily 10–1, 2–5; Jul–Aug, 10–1, 2–7
1, 6
Free
Royal Mile (➤ 24–5)

THE UNIVERSITY OF EDINBURGH ✪

The University of Edinburgh was founded in 1582. Its buildings are centred around Old College, designed by Robert Adam in 1789. Near by lies George Square, home to arts and science, with a few fine Georgian houses still huddled beneath the monstrous 1960s campus building. The McEwan Hall is used for ceremonial occasions, while the classical Reid Concert Hall also houses the Historic Instrument Collection. You can visit several of the university's buildings: the Playfair Library, one of Edinburgh's finest classical interiors, is the pick of the bunch.

29D2
University of Edinburgh Centre, 7–11 Nicolson Street
0131 650 2252
Mon–Fri, 9–5
3, 7, 21, 36
Good
Free
The Meadows (➤ 55); Museum of Scotland (➤ 19)

VICTORIA STREET

⊕⊕

- 29D2
- Victoria Street
- 1, 28, 40
- Good
- The Grassmarket (► 47); Scottish Parliament (► 66)

The steep curve of Victoria Street links the Grassmarket with George IV Bridge and the Royal Mile. It's a cobbled street lined with some of Edinburgh's most individual and beguiling shops. As you walk down, look up to your right at the old tenements clinging to the precipitous slopes beneath the Royal Mile. This area is the West Bow, once the processional way into the Old Town, and the former route from Castlehill to the Grassmarket. Walk along Victoria Terrace, perched above the roofs of Victoria Street, to experience the atmosphere of this part of town.

THE WATER OF LEITH

- 28A4
- Runs from Balerno to Leith with access at different points
- Balerno 43, 47; Leith 1, 10, 16, 25
- Few
- Dean Village (► 41); Leith (► 54); Stockbridge (► 68)

Water of Leith Visitor Centre
- 24 Lanark Road (near Balerno)
- ☎ 0131 455 7367

The Water of Leith runs for more than 32km (20 miles) through a string of suburbs and Edinburgh itself to reach the Firth of Forth at Leith. Most of its course is a gentle meander, with more dramatic scenery at Dean (► 41), where the water has carved its way through a deep gorge. For hundreds of years the banks were lined with mills, with up to 80 on the bottom stretch in the early 1800s. A 21-km (13-mile) walkway follows the path of the river from Balerno to Leith, a good way to explore the area. The nicest stretch by far centres around Stockbridge (► 68); this agreeable walk (► 67) gives access upriver to the Scottish National Gallery of Modern Art (► 65) and downstream to the Royal Botanic Garden (► 23). Alternatively, follow the last stages of the Water through Leith, where you'll see some 17th- and 18th-century warehouses and merchants' houses near the Water's end at the docks.

Above: *colourful façades in Victoria Street front some of Edinburgh's most interesting shops*

Right: *many of the buildings along the Water of Leith recall its early industrial past*

WATERLOO PLACE ☆

Waterloo Place is the continuation of Princes Street to the east, a superbly balanced example of grandiose neo-classical architectural design. If you're hurrying through on your way to Calton Hill, pause to admire the rhythm of the soaring façades of its buildings. Waterloo Place runs through the Old Calton cemetery; here are buried some of the major figures of the Scottish Enlightenment such as the philosopher David Hume, and there's a fine view back to the castle. More prosaically, the bottom of the place gives access to the St James Centre, a hideous block-like concrete structure housing a wide range of shops. The public outcry following its construction probably did more than anything else to further the cause of conservation during the early 1970s.

✚ 29D3
✉ Waterloo Place
🍴 Bars and cafés (£)
🚌 26, 33, 40, 85
♿ Good
↔ Calton Hill (➤ 35)

DID YOU KNOW?

Some scenes from the cult film *Trainspotting* (1995) were shot in Edinburgh, where the action takes place, though most locations are in Glasgow. Look out for the St James Oyster Bar near Waterloo Place; this is where Renton runs into a car in the opening scene. *Shallow Grave* (1995), from the same production team, was also partly filmed in the city.

The airy interior of Princes Mall shelters the capital's shoppers whatever the weather

WAVERLEY MARKET (PRINCES MALL) ☆

Waverley Market, recently renamed Princes Mall, was opened in 1984 and occupies the site of the old vegetable market, which was displaced in the 19th century by a market hall used for concerts and exhibitions. This familiar landmark was demolished to make way for today's functional granite structure, whose flat roof, level with Princes Street, houses Edinburgh's main tourist office. The speciality shopping mall, with over 80 shops, is a good place to hunt for more unusual clothes and gifts. There's a convenient food court as well, good for a quick lunch in between sightseeing.

✚ 29D3
✉ Princes Street East End
☎ 0131 557 3759
🕐 Mon–Wed, Fri, Sat 8:30–6; Thu 8:30–7; Sun 11–5
🍴 Range of restaurants and cafés (£–££)
🚌 2, 10, 15, 26, 33, 45
♿ Very good
↔ Princes Street (➤ 59); Scott Monument (➤ 26)

Around Edinburgh

Using Edinburgh as a base, it's possible to get a real taste of the immense diversity of Scotland – its spectacular scenery, dramatic coastline, forbidding castles and grand mansions, ancient towns and attractive villages. Within a few hours' drive, striking north or south, you can experience a wealth of different sights, which do much to put the city into perspective as the country's capital.

Central Scotland is home to the majority of Scots, with good roads and transport links, much of Scotland's industry and an increasing sense of purpose and hope for the future. Equally, some of the country's best agricultural land lies near at hand, while the hills, lochs and rivers offer the chance to appreciate a sense of space found in few other areas. Glasgow's dynamism stands in contrast to the tranquillity of the Fife and Borders villages, while its rich cultural life and history are further assets which will add to your Edinburgh experience.

> *' Scotland is the country above all others that I have seen, in which a man of imagination may carve out his own pleasures... '*
>
> DOROTHY WORDSWORTH,
> Journal,
> August 1803

The interior of Glasgow School of Art, designed by Charles Rennie Mackintosh

✚ 78B3
ℹ 11 George Square
☎ 0141 204 4400
website:
TourismGlasgow
@ggcvtb.org.uk
Airport Tourist
Information Centre,
Glasgow International
Airport, Paisley
☎ 0141 848 4440

Glasgow

Glasgow, Scotland's largest city, lies a mere 80km (50 miles) from Edinburgh, a city so different in heritage, atmosphere and style that it might as well be 800km away. Industrial Glasgow, decaying 40 years ago, is now one of Britain's most go-ahead cities, with superb 19th-century architecture – it was voted 1999's City of Architecture – and a tangible atmosphere of dynamism. Go there to enjoy the contrast with Edinburgh, the buzz of its designer shops, restaurants and museums, and the wonderful friendliness of its people.

What to See in Glasgow

BURRELL COLLECTION ✪✪✪

✉ 2060 Pollokshaws Road
☎ 0141 287 2550
🕐 Mon–Thu, Sat 10–5; Fri,
Sun 11–5
🍴 Restaurant and café
(£–££)
🚉 Pollokshaws East
♿ Excellent
✋ Free

Glasgow inherited Sir William Burrell's outstanding art collections in 1944, but it was not until 1983 that a suitable home was built for them, a clean-lined stone and glass structure in Bellahouston Park on the south side of the city. Here you'll find paintings, furniture, sculpture and ceramics, architectural fragments and superb Egyptian, Greek, Roman and Asiatic pieces of all sorts. Art-lovers journey to Glasgow specifically to see the collection, so you need to allow plenty of time. The highlight is the huge Warwick Vase, a 2nd-century Roman marble urn.

A superb doorway installed as a focal point in the galleries of the Burrell Collection

BUCHANAN STREET AND PRINCES SQUARE ✪✪

✉ Buchanan Street
🍴 Range of restaurants,
bars and cafés (£–£££)
🚉 Buchanan Street
♿ Very good
↔ George Square
(▶ opposite)

If you're looking for stylish, up-market shopping, head for pedestrianised Buchanan Street, which runs north from Argyle Street, home of the St Enoch Centre, Europe's largest glass-roofed shopping centre. Princes Square is accessed from Buchanan Street; this ultra-modern shopping mall, all glass, wood and designer stores, owes more than a nod to Charles Rennie Mackintosh.

CHARLES RENNIE MACKINTOSH TRAIL ✪✪

Fans of Glasgow's most famous architect, born here in 1868, can track down some of the best examples of his work, stylistically an entirely original blend of Arts and Crafts, art nouveau and Scottish. Head for the Glasgow School of Art, still a working school and one of his best-known designs, before taking in the famous Willow Tea Rooms in Sauchiehall Street and Bellahouston Park's House for an Art Lover. Kelvingrove Museum and The Hunterian Museum each contain Mackintosh interiors, furniture and decorative objects.

🛈 Mackintosh tours are organised by the Charles Rennie Mackintosh Society, Queens Cross Church, 870 Garscube Road ☎ 0141 946 6600

Shopping is a pleasure amid the elegance of Princes Square

GEORGE SQUARE ✪✪

Glasgow's grandiose George Square epitomises the city's 19th-century industrial prosperity. Its wide expanse is dominated by the massive block of the magnificent City Chambers, which has an Italian Renaissance-style façade that gives a taste of the splendours within. Sir Walter Scott looms over it all from a 24m column, and 10 other statues include those of Queen Victoria, Robert Burns and James Watt. Southeast from the square spreads the 'Merchant City', once the trading centre, now a booming area of chic bars and designer stores.

✉ George Square
🍴 Range of restaurants, bars and cafés (£–£££)
Ⓟ Buchanan Street
♿ Very good
↔ Buchanan Street (► opposite)

GLASGOW CATHEDRAL ✪

Set in the oldest part of Glasgow, the cathedral was founded by St Mungo in the 6th century; you'll find the saint's tomb in the crypt. Parts of the Gothic building date from the 12th century, making it one of Scotland's oldest churches. The square outside was the city's first public hanging place. Near by you'll find the superb Necropolis, one of Europe's grandest cemeteries, where Glasgow's merchant princes erected monuments to befit their aspirations.

✉ Castle Street
☎ 0141 552 6891
🕐 Mon–Sat 9:30–4:30, Sun 2–4:30 (later in summer)
Ⓟ High Street
♿ Very good
🎟 Free
↔ St Mungo Museum of Religious Life (► 76)

⊠ Argyle Street
☎ 0141 287 2699
🕐 Mon–Thu, Sat 10–5; Fri, Sun 11–5
🍴 Café (£–££)
🚇 Kelvinhall
♿ Very good
💷 Free

KELVINGROVE ART GALLERY AND MUSEUM ✪

The red sandstone palace housing the art gallery went up in 1901 for the International Exhibition; today it's the home of the varied city collections, which range from natural history to paintings. The paintings are upstairs and include some monumental Victorian history pictures, as well as a range of Scottish art; look out for the Glasgow Boys' School work. Mackintosh fans will enjoy *Glasgow 1900*, a permanent display of furniture and art setting the architect in the context of turn-of-the-century Glasgow.

⊠ Glasgow Green
☎ 0141 554 0223
🕐 Mon–Thu, Sat 10–5, Fri, Sun 11–5
🚇 Bridgeton
♿ Good
💷 Free

PEOPLE'S PALACE ✪✪

There's no better place to get a feel for the social history of Glasgow than in the 1898 People's Palace, which has exhibitions devoted to all aspects of everyday and working life in the city. The museum has undergone a refit, making the displays more interactive and visitor-friendly. The splendid adjoining Winter Gardens were badly damaged by a fire in 1998.

A detail from the exterior of the People's Palace exemplifies the mercantile confidence of 19th-century Glasgow

⊠ 2 Castle Street
☎ 0141 553 2557
🕐 Mon–Thu, Sat 10–5; Fri, Sun 11–5
🚇 High Street
♿ Very good
💷 Free
↔ Glasgow Cathedral (► 75)

ST MUNGO MUSEUM OF RELIGIOUS LIFE AND ✪✪
ART (INCLUDING PROVAN'S LORDSHIP)

Christianity is only one of the six major world religions covered by this museum's fascinating displays, which include stained glass, and artefacts from India, China, Africa and North America. Most people come here for one painting alone; Salvador Dali's striking and enigmatic *Christ of St John of the Cross*.

⊠ Sauchiehall Street
🍴 Range of restaurants, bars and cafés (£–£££)
🚌 11, 18, 21, 23
♿ Good

SAUCHIEHALL STREET ✪

Sauchiehall Street runs from Kelvingrove Park almost as far as George Square, but it's the thought of the eastern stretch that brings a tear to the eye of homesick Glaswegians. This bustling, crowded, noisy shopping street means home to the city's people, and a stroll down its pedestrianised section is an essential part of the Glasgow experience.

What to See Around Edinburgh

ABBOTSFORD HOUSE ⬤⬤
Whether or not you've read Sir Walter Scott's Waverley novels, his neo-Baronial mansion home at Abbotsford is fascinating. Built between 1811 and 1823, this extraordinary edifice and its contents tell us as much about Scott's fascination with Scottish history as do his books. Doors, arches and ceilings are replicas of the writer's favourites from all over Scotland and the house still contains his historical collection and his 9,000-volume library. You can see Rob Roy's sword and sporran and a purse made by Flora MacDonald among the wealth of ephemera. Most evocative, perhaps, is the small study with its desk and chair where he wrote so many of his books. Scott died at Abbotsford in 1832.

➕ 79E2
✉ Abbotsford House, Melrose
☎ 01896 752043
🕐 Mar–Oct, Mon–Sat 10–5; Mar–May, Oct, Sun 2–5; Jun–Sep, 10–5
🍴 Café £ Apr–Sep
🚌 From Galashiels or Melrose, alight at Tweedbank
♿ Few
💷 Expensive
↔ Eildon Hills (▶ 82)

THE BASS ROCK ⬤
Visitors to North Berwick (▶ 84) can't miss the prominent silhouette of the Bass Rock, a volcanic plug rising 107m above the sea to the northeast. Once used as a prison island, its main inhabitants today are a huge colony of gannets as well as many other seabirds. A boat trip out to the rock on a fine day makes an excellent change of pace after an overdose of city sightseeing (▶ 121).

➕ 79E3
✉ 5km (3 miles) northeast of North Berwick
☎ Mr Marr 01620 892838
💷 Moderate

The distinctive outline of the Bass Rock

DALMENY HOUSE ⬤
Dalmeny House, home of the Earl of Rosebery, was designed in 1815 and is the first example of a Gothic Tudor Revival house in Scotland. Most visitors come to admire the superb interior furnishings, which came from the Rothschild collection at Mentmore. Highlights include the Goya-designed tapestries, fine French furniture made for Louis XIV and an entire room devoted to mementoes of Napoleon. Dalmeny's beautifully-kept grounds stretch along the shore of the Firth of Forth.

➕ 79D3
✉ South Queensferry
☎ 0131 331 1888
🕐 Jul–Aug, Mon and Tue 12–5:30, Sun 1–5:30
🚌 Bus from St Andrews Square
♿ Few
💷 Expensive
↔ Hopetoun House (▶ 83)

77

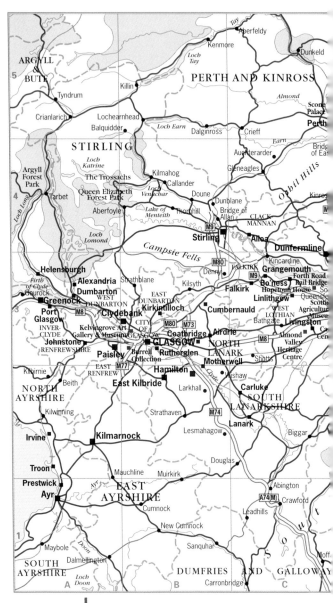

CENTRAL SCOTLAND

Lunan Bay

Forfar

Blairgowrie

Coupar Angus

Arbroath

Carnoustie

Sidlaw Hills

Dundee   DUNDEE CITY

Firth of Tay   Newport-on-Tay

St Andrews Bay

Scottish
Deer
Centre   *Eden*   St Andrews

Auchtermuchty   Cupar

Ceres   Fife Ness

FIFE   Crail

Falkland   Lower
Largo   Kellie
Castle   *East Neuk of Fife*

*Loch
Leven*   Glenrothes   Leven   Elie   Scottish
Fisheries
Museum   Isle of May

Cowdenbeath   Buckhaven

Kirkcaldy   Burntisland

Inver-
keithing   Bass Rock

Deep Sea World   *Firth of Forth*   North Berwick   Tantallon Castle

Dalmeny House   Dirleton   Dunbar

Newhaven   Leith   East Linton

EDINBURGH   Cockburnspath

Portobello   Haddington   St Abb's Head

Lauriston Castle   Musselburgh   Lennoxlove House

rstorphine   Morning   Craigmillar Castle   Pencaitland   Eyemouth

alerno   side   Duddingston

swanston   Butterfly Farm   Dalkeith   EAST
LOTHIAN   *Meikle
Says
Law
533m*   *Lammermuir*   Grantshouse

Centre   Bonnyrigg

Penicuik   Rosslyn
Chapel   Scottish Mining Museum   *Hills*

*Pentland
Hills*   MIDLOTHIAN   Duns

Gladhouse
Reservoir   Berwick-upon-Tweed

West
Linton   *Moorfoot
Hills*   Lauder   Greenlaw

Peebles   Stow   Gordon   *Tweed*

Tweed   Neidpath
Castle   Innerleithen   Galashiels   Coldstream

Drumelzier   Traquair
House   Abbotsford
House   Melrose   Kelso

Selkirk Hills   Dryburgh
Abbey

Eildon

Tweed

BORDERS   *Teviot*

*White
omb
22m*   St Mary's
Loch   *The Cheviot Hills*   816m

Ettrick   Hawick   Jedburgh

Teviothead   Carter
Bar   ENGLAND

| | D | | E | | F |

0   10   20 kms
0   5   10 miles

Dirleton Castle
- ✚ 79E3
- ✉ Dirleton, near North Berwick
- ☎ 01620 850330
- 🕐 Apr–Sep, daily 9:30–6:30; Oct–Mar, 9:30–4:30
- 🚌 Buses from St Andrew Square
- ♿ Few
- 👆 Moderate

Dirleton's lovely gardens at their summertime best

- ✚ 79E2
- ✉ Near Melrose
- ☎ 01835 822381
- 🕐 Apr–Sep, daily 9:30–6:30; Oct–Mar, Mon–Sat 9:30–4:30, Sun 2–4:30
- ♿ Few
- 👆 Moderate

Crail Museum and Heritage Centre
- ✚ 79E4
- ✉ Marketgate, Crail
- ☎ 01333 450869
- 🕐 Easter and Jun–Sep, Mon–Sat 10–1 and 2–5, Sun 2–5
- ♿ Few
- 👆 Free

Kellie Castle and Gardens
- ✚ 79E4
- ✉ Near Pittenweem
- ☎ 01333 720271
- 🕐 Easter and May–Sep, daily 1:30–5:30; Oct, Sat and Sun only 1:30–5:30
- 🍴 Tea room (£–££)
- ♿ Few
- 👆 Moderate (free to National Trust and National Trust for Scotland members)

DIRLETON ✪✪

Near the shores of the Firth of Forth, picture-postcard

Dirleton, with its trim cottages and flower-crammed gardens, clusters around its village green with the ruins of an ancient **castle** rising to one side. Built in the 13th century, the castle was repeatedly rebuilt on its natural rock platform until its final destruction in 1650. Today, it's one of the area's most romantic ruins, enhanced by its lovely gardens, first recorded in the 16th century.

DRYBURGH ABBEY ✪✪

The Borders are well endowed with abbey ruins, but it's perhaps Dryburgh's tranquil position on the wooded banks of the River Tweed that give it its special allure. Nothing survives of the original 7th-century foundation and today's remains of abbey, chapter house and conventual buildings date mainly from the 12th–14th centuries. The ruins contain the grave of Sir Walter Scott, who is buried here as an ancestral right from the days when his great-grand-father owned the abbey site.

THE EAST NEUK OF FIFE ✪✪

A string of picturesque coastal villages, rich in vernacular architecture, snug harbours and blessed with sandy beaches, runs along Fife's southeast shore. James II called the East Neuk (or promontory) 'the golden fringe on a beggar's mantle', a rich trading and fishing area in his otherwise impoverished kingdom. The main towns are Crail, Pittenweem, Anstruther, Largo and Elie, all very different and each preserving its own character and charm. A day spent exploring this area offers everything from watersports and golf to museums and castles. Highlights include the **Crail Heritage Centre** and **Kellie Castle and Gardens**, 5km (3 miles) inland from Pittenweem.

DID YOU KNOW?

The three cantilevered spans of the Forth Rail Bridge are perfectly complemented by the graceful lines of the Road Bridge just upstream. The rail bridge was completed in 1890, using 55,880 tonnes of steel, 18,112cu m of granite, 1,755cu m of masonry and 8 million rivets. The road bridge measures 1,829m and is one of the world's largest suspension bridges.

A Drive Exploring Fife

Leave Leven on the A915 heading east and through Lundin Links; take the turn-off signposted Lower Largo.

Lower Largo, once a fishing port and today an attractive little holiday village, was the birthplace of Alexander Selkirk (1676–1721), the model for Daniel Defoe's Robinson Crusoe; his statue stands by the harbour.

Return to the main road and branch right in Upper Largo on to the A917 to Elie. Continue through St Monans and Pittenweem to Anstruther and Crail.

St Monans, Pittenweem, Anstruther and Crail are East Neuk villages (► opposite). To explore each of them you will need to turn off the main road and follow the signs to their harbours. Each has its own charm and character, with narrow streets lined with the red-roofed, crow-stepped gabled houses that typify Fife vernacular architecture.

From Crail head north on the A917 to St Andrews (► 85). Leave St Andrews on the A91 to Cupar. Leave Cupar on the A91 signposted Auchtermuchty and M90.

Cupar, the old county town, lies in the rolling agricultural land of the River Eden valley, known as the Howe of Fife. Scattered with pretty villages such as Ceres (on the B939 southeast of Cupar), it's worth lingering here if there's time. Children will enjoy the Scottish Deer Centre (on the A91) where they can ride in a trailer to see magnificent red deer. The tiny royal burgh of Auchtermuchty was once a royal hunting base; it has some fine 18th-century houses dating from its prosperous weaving past.

In Auchtermuchty turn left on the B936 to Falkland (► 82).

Distance
77km (48 miles)

Time
2 hours without stops or a full day with visits

Start point
Leven
✚ 79D4

End point
Falkland
✚ 79D4

Lunch
The Doll's House Restaurant (££)
✉ 3 Church Square, St Andrews
☎ 01334 477422

St Monan's Church, seen against a typical east coast background of sky, sea and clustered fishermen's houses

Trimontium Exhibition
- 79E2
- Ormiston Institute, The Square, Melrose
- 01896 822651
- Apr–Oct, Mon–Fri 10:30–4:30; Sat and Sun 10:30–1 and 2–4:30
- Good
- Cheap

Falkland Palace
- 79D4
- 01337 857397
- Apr–Oct, Mon–Sat 11–5:30; Sun 1:30–5:30
- Few
- Expensive (Free to National Trust and National Trust for Scotland members)
- East Neuk of Fife (➤ 80); St Andrews (➤ 85)

Falkland (below); (inset) a 17th-century plaque

THE EILDON HILLS

South of Melrose and the River Tweed rise the rounded shapes of the three peaks of the Eildon Hills, a distinctive Borders landmark. Formed by volcanic activity 300 million years ago, smoothed by ice and weathering, the hills are surrounded by legend. King Arthur is said to have been buried beneath the Eildons after his death in a great battle, and to lie among his sleeping warriors and knights, all of them ready to rise and defend their country if called upon again. More easily provable is the Roman presence; they named the hills Trimontium and built an important fort and township. You can learn more at the Trimontium exhibition in nearby Melrose, or even climb the hills, a 2–3-hour circular walk with far-reaching views over the scenery of the Borders.

FALKLAND

The royal burgh of Falkland is one of Scotland's prettiest small towns, its spacious square dominated by its superb Scottish Renaissance **palace** and its cobbled streets lined with attractive 18th-century weavers' cottages. Falkland lay at the centre of the 15th-century Stuart hunting lands, and the royal hunting lodge was transformed into a palace by James IV and James V between 1501 and 1541. It fell into neglect from 1715 until the late 19th century. The beautifully restored King's Bedchamber and the Queen's Room lie in the East Range, with the serene and lovely Chapel Royal to the south. Lawns, trees and well-stocked herbaceous borders surround the palace, sweeping down to the royal tennis court of 1539, the oldest one in Britain still in use.

The lawns around the massive walls of Linlithgow Palace make a good picnic place

HADDINGTON

Set in the fertile land between the Lammermuir Hills and the coast, the royal burgh of Haddington boasts no less than 130 buildings listed as being of historical or architectural interest, a fine late medieval parish church, a beguilingly oddly shaped square as well as galleries, museums and enticing shops. Don't miss the alabaster Elizabethan monuments in the Lauderdale Aisle in St Mary's Church, which also houses the tomb of Jane Carlyle, wife of the historian Thomas Carlyle; there's a **museum** in her childhood home. Outside town, Lennoxlove House, seat of the Dukes of Hamilton, is one of Scotland's grandest houses.

Jane Welsh Carlyle Museum
- 79E3
- 2 Lodge Street
- 01620 823738
- Apr–Sep, Wed–Sat 2–5
- Few
- Cheap

HOPETOUN HOUSE

Hopetoun House is often considered to be the grandest house in Scotland. Its first phase was designed by William Bruce for the newly rich Hope family and built between 1699 and 1702. William Adam was brought in as architect in 1721, and it is to his plans that we owe today's magnificent façade with its sweeping colonnades and flanking pavilions. The carved and painted state apartments contain good pictures and furniture, and the great house, still the home of the Hopes, now the Marquesses of Linlithgow, is surrounded by rolling parkland.

- 78C3
- South Queensferry
- 0131 331 2451
- Apr–Sep, daily 10–5:30;
  Oct, Sat and Sun only
- Restaurant and tea room
  (£–££)
- Good
- Expensive

LINLITHGOW

Visitors to Linlithgow should head first to the **Linlithgow Story**, which relates the history of this medieval industrial centre and royal burgh. Today the **palace** is the main draw, a well-preserved loch-side 15th-century ruin, where Mary, Queen of Scots was born in 1542. Next door stands St Michael's Church, rebuilt in 1424 and topped by an eye-catching aluminium tower in the 1960s. The town is liberally dotted with fine 17th-century buildings, while outside stands the House of the Binns, a 17th-century house bridging the architectural gap between fortified stronghold and mansion.

- 78C3

Linlithgow Palace
- 01506 842896
- Apr–Sep, daily 9:30–6:30;
  Oct–Mar, daily 9:30–4:30
- Moderate

The Linlithgow Story
- 143 High Street
- 01506 670677
- Easter–Oct, Mon–Sat
  10–5; Sun 1–4

83

79D2

✉ Peebles
☎ 01721 720333
🕓 Easter–Sep, Mon–Sat 11–5; Sun 1–5
♿ Few
🚻 Moderate
↔ Peebles (► below)

79E3

North Berwick Museum
✉ School Road
☎ 01620 895457
🕓 Apr–Oct, daily 11–5

Scottish Seabird Centre
✉ North Berwick Harbour
☎ 01620 890202
🕓 Apr–Oct, daily; phone for times and winter opening
♿ Excellent

79D2

Tourist Information Centre
✉ High Street
☎ 01721 720138
🕓 Jan–Dec
↔ Neidpath Castle (► above)

Neidpath Castle – the epitome of everything a castle should be

NEIDPATH CASTLE ✪

It's a pleasant walk from the centre of Peebles to Neidpath Castle, an imposing turreted structure gloriously set on a rocky outcrop above a bend of the River Tweed. This 14th-century L-plan tower house has passed from the Frasers via the Hays, Douglases and Scotts to the Earls of Wemyss, who restored it in the 19th century. Children enjoy exploring the castle with its pit prison and small museum, and you can picnic in the grounds.

NORTH BERWICK ✪

North Berwick, once a fishing and trading port, is now a prosperous commuter town and holiday resort, with solid Victorian buildings, a bustling harbour, a renowned golf course, good shops, and sandy beaches and impressive coastline nearby. The town's **museum** will fill you in on local history (plenty of witches' tales), and the energetic might tackle Berwick Law, a 187m high volcanic rock formation behind the town. Birdwatchers should head for the **Scottish Seabird Centre**, a brand-new attraction where you can see, study and learn more about the birds of the Bass Rock (► 77) and surrounding coastline.

PEEBLES ✪

Long popular with holiday-makers, Peebles is a clean and couthy riverside town beautifully set beside the Tweed and girdled with gently rolling hills. Antiquities include two ancient churches, a 14th-century mercat cross and a graceful five-arched bridge, first built in the 15th century. The town has been a wool-manufacturing centre for many years, and you'll find plenty of wool and knitwear shops and some interesting antique shops. The town's literary connections are strong; William and Robert Chambers, the founders of Chambers Dictionary, were born here, Robert Louis Stevenson lived here as a child, and John Buchan spent happy summers here with his family.

ROSSLYN CHAPEL ⭐⭐

For a glimpse of some of Britain's finest medieval stone carving head for Rosslyn Chapel, just south of Edinburgh. Founded in 1447 by William Sinclair, the 3rd Earl of Orkney, the chapel was intended to form part of a huge collegiate church dedicated to St Michael, which was never built. Only 21m (69 feet) long, the entire chapel is profusely carved with intricate and sophisticated sculptures, entwined with flowers and foliage. Most famous is the so-called Prentice Pillar, said to have been carved by an apprentice while his master was away; so fine was the pupil's work that his master killed him out of jealousy on his return.

ST ANDREWS ⭐⭐⭐

It's every golfer's dream to visit St Andrews, a historic and beautiful town, the home of Scotland's oldest university (1412) and the country's ancient ecclesiastical centre. Legend recounts that it was founded by a shipwrecked Greek monk carrying relics of the saint. By the 12th century, when the construction of the cathedral started, St Andrews was already a leading religious centre. The massive cathedral was destroyed during the Reformation, but nearby St Rule's Tower still stands, a great place for a view over the town's medieval street plan. Clinging to a coastal headland near the cathedral is the castle, worth a visit for its atmosphere and bottle-neck dungeon alone, while golfers should head for the **British Golf Museum**. You can take your children to the fascinating **Sea Life Centre**, or explore the **museum**, browse in the town's excellent shops or simply take a stroll along the sandy, and often windswept, beaches.

79D3
✉ Roslin, Midlothian
☎ 0131 440 2159
🕐 Mon–Sat 10–5; Sun 12–4.45
♿ Good
👋 Moderate

Above left: the Royal and Ancient Clubhouse, St Andrews
Above: carvings, Rosslyn

79E4

British Golf Museum
✉ Bruce Embankment
☎ 01334 478880
🕐 Phone for times
♿ Very good
👋 Moderate

St Andrews Museum
✉ Kinburn Park, Double Dykes Road
☎ 01334 412690
🕐 Apr–Sep, daily 10–5; Oct–Mar, Mon–Fri 10:30–4, Sat and Sun 12:30–5
♿ Good
👋 Free

Sea Life Centre
✉ The Scores
☎ 01334 474786
🕐 Apr–Oct, 10–6; phone for winter opening hours
♿ Good
👋 Expensive

DID YOU KNOW?

'Haar', a chill and damp summer sea-mist, sometimes occurs along the coast east of Edinburgh and even in the city itself. It is usually a sign that there is brilliant sunshine just a few kilometres inland.

A Walk Around St Andrews

Start at the cathedral and head west down South Street.

South Street has some fine examples of 17th- and 18th-century houses, many of them still backed by long, narrow gardens, a relic of the medieval town. On the left you'll see St Mary's, the university's theological college, with gracious buildings set around a courtyard and lawns beyond. Diagonally opposite stands Holy Trinity Church, a fine re-creation of a medieval town church still retaining its 15th-century tower.

Opposite the far end of Madras College grounds turn right down Bell Street, then cross the road to continue along Greyfriars Gardens to North Street. Turn left down the hill, cross the road, and right into Golf Place.

History gives way here to golf, sand and sea, with the imposing clubhouse of the Royal and Ancient Golf Club straight ahead, and the links stretching along the sea. The British Golf Museum and Sea Life Centre lie just off the Scores (➤ 85).

From the bottom of Golf Place turn right along the Scores, following the road all the way along to the castle. Opposite the castle head straight up North Castle Street and turn right down North Street.

The right side of the street is lined with university buildings; take a look at the fine quadrangle of St Salvator's College and the university chapel.

Opposite St Salvator's turn left into College Street; this leads to spacious Market Street; cross over and continue straight ahead down Church Street to turn left to rejoin South Street and return to the cathedral.

The size and scale of the ruins of St Andrews Cathedral inspire awe

Distance
3 km (1.8miles)

Start/end point
St Andrews Cathedral

Lunch
The North Point Café (££)
✉ 24 North Street,
St Andrews
☎ 01334 473997

The gateway to historic St Mary's College

IN · PRINCIPIO · ERAT · VERBVM

SCONE PALACE 😊😊

Scone Palace, the home of the Earls of Mansfield, dates mainly from the early 19th century, and is one of the grandest of Scotland's stately homes. In its grounds stands Moot Hill, the ancient coronation site of the Scottish monarchs, where Robert the Bruce was crowned and where the Stone of Destiny was kept for 500 years. The present Gothic-style building went up around an earlier palace in 1803 and contains superb collections of furniture, pictures and rare porcelain and ivories. Scone is surrounded with lovely grounds, where children will enjoy the maze, animals and playground.

STIRLING 😊😊

Strategically situated near the Highland line, with the River Forth's lowest bridging point to hand, the rocky outcrop of historic Stirling was the obvious place to build a castle. It still stands, with wide views over the town and some lovely Renaissance buildings, which include the magnificent Great Hall and Chapel Royal, much used by the Stuart monarchs. Scotland's history is further celebrated outside town by the **Wallace Monument**, a 67m tower built in 1869 to commemorate William Wallace, the Braveheart, and his victory over the English at the Battle of Stirling Bridge in 1297. 3km (2 miles) to the south you can learn more Scots history at **Bannockburn**, scene of the rout of Edward II's army by Robert the Bruce in 1314. The town itself spreads down from the **castle**; here, the streets containing the older buildings, which include the tolbooth, old town jail, and 15th-century Holy Rude church, give way to Victorian development and modern shopping centres serving Stirling's prosperous agricultural hinterland.

+ 78C5
✉ Scone, Perth
☎ 01738 552300
🕐 Easter–Oct, 9:30–5:15
🍴 Restaurant and café (£–££)
♿ Very good
✋ Expensive

Below: *the treasures of Scone displayed to perfection in a graceful Gothic gallery*

+ 78B4

Bannockburn Heritage Centre
☎ 01786 812664
🕐 Site daily all year; check times for Heritage Centre
♿ Good
✋ Moderate

National Wallace Monument
☎ 01786 472140
🕐 Phone to check

Stirling Castle
☎ 01768 450000
🕐 Daily Apr–Sep, 9:30–6; Oct–Mar, 9:30–5
🍴 Restaurant and café (£–££)
♿ Good
✋ Expensive

79E3
Near North Berwick
01620 892727
Apr–Sep, daily 9:30–6:30;
Oct–Mar, Mon–Wed and
Sat 9:30–4:30, Thu
9:30–12, Fri and Sun
2–4:30
Few
Moderate
North Berwick (➤ 84)

TANTALLON CASTLE

The castle at Tantallon stands on a promontory high above the sea, the entire headland protected by massive walls and earthworks. Behind, a spectacular exposed coastal view opens up, with the Bass Rock in the background. One of Scotland's most evocative ruins, Tantallon was built in the 14th century as a castle of enclosure, and comprises little more than walls, towers and defences 'enclosing' a grassy platform on the cliffs above the pounding sea. Built of local red rock, its 15m thick walls are flanked by towers and pierced by a central gatehouse-keep. The stronghold was besieged and blockaded several times and passed in and out of the Douglas family's ownership down the years. In 1651 it was attacked by English forces under the command of General Monk, and its medieval defences proved no match for state-of-the-art 17th-century ordnance.

> ### DID YOU KNOW?
>
> The Scottish flag, a diagonal white cross on a blue background, is known as The Saltire. Its colours are traditionally associated with St Andrew, Scotland's patron saint. Legend tells that a white cloud cross was seen against the blue sky during the 9th-century Battle of Athelstaneford, when the Northumbrians were defeated, and St Andrew and his symbol were adopted in thanksgiving.

79D2
Innerleithen
01896 830323
Apr–May and Sep,
12:30–5:30; Jun–Aug,
10:30–5:30; Oct, Fri–Sun
12:30–5:30
Restaurant and café
(£–££)
Good
Expensive
Traquair Beer Festival,
May; Traquair Fair, Aug

TRAQUAIR HOUSE

Traquair claims to be Scotland's oldest inhabited house, a peaceful turreted building set around a formal courtyard, once a royal hunting lodge given by James III to the Earl of Buchan, whose descendants own the house today. It was mostly rebuilt in the 17th century, when considerable changes were made and the wings and courtyard added. An avenue of trees leads to the house, fronted by a pair of gates known as the 'Steekit Yetts', or 'shut gates', which have been closed for more than 200 years; some say they were shut behind Bonnie Prince Charlie and will not be opened until the Stuarts reign again, others that they await the arrival of a new Countess of Traquair.

From Stirling to the Heart of The Trossachs

From Stirling (➤ 87) take the A9 through Bridge of Allan to Dunblane, then west on the A820 to Doune. Join the A84 at Doune.

Doune lies at the threshold of the Highlands. The impressive 14th-century castle, one of Scotland's finest medieval strongholds, is open all year.

Continue on the A84 to Callander (➤ 90). Leave Callander on the A84 and after 2km (1 mile) turn left at Kilmahog on to the A821.

The Highland scenery of Loch Vennachar, with the wooded hills of the Queen Elizabeth Forest Park behind, now starts to open up.

Continue on the A821 to Brig o' Turk and along the shores of Loch Achray.

You are now approaching the heart of the Trossachs (➤ 90).

Turn right at the head of Loch Achray to Loch Katrine Pier (➤ 90). Retrace the road and turn right on the A821 towards Aberfoyle (➤ 90).

The road climbs through forested hills to the Duke's Pass, where there's a viewpoint with a spectacular panorama over the whole area.

From Aberfoyle take the A81 past the Lake of Menteith and then branch right on the A873 to Thornhill.

The Lake of Menteith is Scotland's only lake; the island houses the ruins of Inchmahome Priory, and can be visited by ferry from Port of Menteith.

Through Thornhill branch left on to the B826 for 4km (2.5 miles), then turn left on the A84 to Doune and return to Stirling via the A820 and A9.

Distance
94km (58 miles)

Time
3 hours without stops, or a full day with visits.

Start/end point
Stirling
✠ 78B4

Lunch
The Byre Inn (£)
✉ Brig o'Turk, by Callander
☎ 01877 376292

Forestry Commission

Queen Elizabeth Forest Park

Information, way-marked trails and picnic places are all available in the well-organised forest park

Opposite: *the romantically sited ruins of Tantallon Castle*

✚ 78B4
Loch Katrine Cruises
☎ 01877 376316
💷 Expensive

Rob Roy and Trossachs Visitor Centre
✉ Ancaster Square, Callander
☎ 01877 330342
🕐 Phone for times
♿ Good

Scottish Wool Centre
✉ off Main Street, Aberfoyle (A821)
☎ 01877 382850
🕐 Mar–Oct, 9:30–6; Nov–Feb, 10–4:30
♿ Very good

Trossachs Discovery Centre
✉ Main Street, Aberfoyle
☎ 01877 82352
🕐 Apr–Oct, daily; Nov–Mar, Sat and Sun only

Scotland's beauty at its best – Loch Achray

THE TROSSACHS ●●●

The heart of the Trossachs centres around a narrow pass leading from Loch Achray, to the west of Callander, to Loch Katrine, a scenically splendid loch in the shadow of Ben A'an, and the historic home of the family of Rob Roy MacGregor. For most visitors, the Trossachs means something much larger; a wonderfully diverse area within easy reach of both Edinburgh and Glasgow, with mountains, lochs and forests, plenty of visitor attractions and outdoor opportunities, where the small towns of Aberfoyle and Callander provide accommodation and a host of tourist facilities.

Either town makes a good starting point for exploring the area; in Aberfoyle, the **Trossachs Discovery Centre** has plenty of information about the natural and cultural heritage, while Callander's **Rob Roy Centre** concentrates on the eponymous folk-hero. Aberfoyle also offers the **Scottish Wool Centre**, a lively attraction telling the story of wool with demonstrations of clipping and working sheepdogs. From each town, scenic roads lead through some of central Scotland's loveliest scenery with a wide choice of walking, cycling and picnic areas. A short detour will bring you to Loch Katrine, where you can take a **cruise** on a Victorian steamship and admire the grandeur surrounding the loch, described by Sir Walter Scott in his poem *The Lady of the Lake*.

To the north lies the tiny hamlet of Balquhidder, where there is a visitor centre and museum; set in impressive mountain scenery, Balquidder is the burial place of Rob Roy MacGregor, his wife and two sons.

Where To...

Above: *tartan and tweed, top buys for many visitors*
Right: *part of a window display at Jenners' famous store*

Edinburgh

Prices

Many Edinburgh restaurants are happy to serve a one- or two-course meal, which is often all you will want. Beer, wine and other alcoholic drinks are expensive in European terms and will increase the meal-cost considerably. Prices quoted are for a three-course meal for one without anything to drink.

£ = budget (up to £12)
££ = moderate (£12–£25)
£££ =expensive (over £25)

All Bar One (££)

Stylish New Town bistro in converted bank building, serving wide selection of imaginative food and wine. Popular place to see and be seen, and the relaxed atmosphere draws shoppers at the weekend.

✉ 29–31 George Street
☎ 0131 226 9971 ⏰ Mon–Thu 12–12; Fri, Sat 12–12:45; Sun 12–11PM 🚌 17, 19, 42

Atrium (££)

A sophisticated, minimalist-décor restaurant housed in the foyer of the Traverse Theatre. It has earned its high reputation with a distinctive range of imaginative Scottish and French dishes.

✉ 10 Cambridge Street
☎ 0131 228 8882 ⏰ Mon–Fri 12–2:30, 6–10:30, Sat 6–10:30. Closed Sun 🚌 9, 10, 11, 35

Ayutthaya (££)

Cosy and relaxed restaurant opposite the Festival Theatre offering an extensive and varied range of authentic Thai dishes; book if you're eating before the theatre.

✉ 14b Nicolson Street
☎ 0131 556 9351 ⏰ Mon–Sun 12–3, 5:30–11 🚌 3, 7, 17, 33

Banns (£)

Cosmopolitan and sophisticated vegetarian food is offered in this popular restaurant off the Royal Mile, with Italian, Thai, Mexican and Japanese influences.

✉ 5 Hunter Square ☎ 0131 226 1112 ⏰ Daily 10AM–11PM 🚌 3, 7, 8

Bar Roma (£)

Popular West End Italian restaurant that has for years served consistently tasty pasta and pizza in generous portions in a happy relaxed atmosphere, great venue for parties.

✉ 39a Queensferry Street
☎ 0131 225 6355 ⏰ Mon–Thu and Sun, 12–12; Fri and Sat 12–12 ⏰ Sun and Mon 10AM–12PM; Tue–Sat 10AM–1AM 🚌 9, 10, 11

Bells Diner (£)

This popular casual Stockbridge diner, an Edinburgh institution, has been producing quality burgers and steaks, desserts and vegeburgers to a satisfied clientele for over 25 years; booking advisable.

✉ 7 St Stephen Street
☎ 0131 225 8116 ⏰ Mon–Fri 6–11, Sat, Sun 12–11 🚌 20, 28

Bonars (£££)

Imaginative food using top-quality, expensive ingredients is served up to the loyal clientele of this pricey restaurant, incongruously decorated with pink chintz. Make sure you leave room for pudding.

✉ 56–8 St Mary's Street
☎ 0131 556 5888 ⏰ Tue–Sat 12–2, 5–10 🚌 1, 6, 60

Café Royal Oyster Bar (£££)

The ornate Victorian décor of this famous New Town institution provides the ideal ambience in which to consume oysters, fish, seafood, Scottish game and vegetarian dishes.

✉ 17a West Register Street
☎ 0131 556 4124 ⏰ Daily 12–2, 7–10 🚌 3, 4, 7, 47

Café St Honore (££)

With a fine blend of Scottish and French influences, this small friendly restaurant, tucked away in a New Town lane, offers simple imaginative dishes with Continental flair. Set menu 5–7PM.

✉ **34 Thistle Street Lane**
☎ **0131 226 2211** ⏰ **Mon–Fri 12–2:15, 5–10; Sat 5–10** 🚌 **3, 4, 7**

Chinese Home Cooking (£)
The quality of the basic traditional Chinese cuisine, simply prepared to a high standard, ensures the popularity of this friendly restaurant, close to the university, with students and locals alike appreciating unbeatable value.

✉ **34 West Preston Street**
☎ **0131 668 4946** ⏰ **Mon–Thu 12–2, 5:30–11; Fri and Sat 12–2, 5:30–11:30; Sun 5:30–11** 🚌 **7, 8, 9**

Cosmo (£££)
This old-fashioned New Town restaurant serves quality 1960s-style Italian cuisine, with wines to match, and over 30 years has acquired an extensive clientele that makes advance booking advisable.

✉ **58a North Castle Street**
☎ **0131 226 6743** ⏰ **Mon–Fri 12:30–2:15, 7–10:45; Sat 7–10:45** 🚌 **13, 17, 19**

Cuisine d'Odile (£)
A little piece of France located in the basement of the Institut Français, with superb cuisine in pleasant surroundings, using local and seasonal ingredients, imaginatively prepared. Bring your own wine, if desired.

✉ **13 Randolph Crescent**
☎ **0131 225 5685** ⏰ **Tue–Sat 12noon–2PM** 🚌 **13, 19, 34, 35**

Dome (£££)
Housed in a former bank, crowned by a hugely impressive glass ceiling, this upmarket bistro has retained the original fittings and serves classic Scottish-

French cuisine for all tastes and appetites.

✉ **14 George Street** ☎ **0131 624 8624** ⏰ **Mon-Sun noon–11** 🚌 **17, 19, 20**

Dubh Prais (££)
A cosy whitewashed cellar houses one of the Royal Mile's better bets, where you'll find traditional Scottish cuisine with the emphasis on fish and seafood, backed up by delicious desserts as well as a fine range of malt whiskies.

✉ **123b, High Street** ☎ **0131 557 5732** ⏰ **Tue–Fri 12–2, 6:30–10:30; Sat 6:30–10:30** 🚌 **1, 6**

Duck's at Marché Noir (££)
Fine New Town French restaurant with classic provincial cooking at its best; nice relaxed ambience and an impressive wine list.

✉ **2–4 Eyre Place** ☎ **0131 558 1608** ⏰ **Mon–Fri 12–2:30, 7–10; Sat 7–10:30; Sun 6:30–9:30** 🚌 **34, 35**

Elephant House (£)
One of the most popular of Edinburgh cafés, this friendly Old Town establishment offers a wide range of light meals and snacks throughout the day, with a tempting array of cakes complementing speciality coffees.

✉ **21 George IV Bridge**
☎ **0131 220 5355** ⏰ **Mon–Thu 8AM–11PM; Fri, Sat 9AM–1AM; Sun 9AM–11PM** 🚌 **23, 27, 28**

Est Est Est (££)
Kids are truly fussed over in this minimalist and stylish New Town establishment. There is a wide range of distinctive Italian dishes – antipasti, pizza and great ice cream are all elegantly presented; booking advisable.

✉ **135a George Street**
☎ **0131 225 2555** ⏰
Mon–Sun noon–11 🚌 **17, 19**

Pub Food

Edinburgh has such a wide choice of restaurants and cafés that many people stick to these, rather than heading for a pub to eat. City-centre pubs do serve food, usually of the ploughman's lunch, pie and chips, or haggis and neeps variety. On the whole, pub food in Scotland is not as imaginative as you may be used to finding in England. In remoter country areas, however, a pub may be your only choice.

Get Stuffed (££)

This old-established small New Town eatery offers generous portions of best Scottish beef, with lamb, chicken, veal and pork also available and some vegetarian dishes, all served in a cosy friendly atmosphere.

✉ 192 Rose Street ☎ 0131 225 2208 🕔 Mon–Fri 12–2, 6–11; Sat 5–11 🚌 3, 4, 17,19

Henderson's Salad Table (£)

This long-established vegetarian restaurant is an Edinburgh institution with a reputation for consistently good salad, soups, hot dishes and puddings and a friendly lively atmosphere; be prepared to queue at busy times.

✉ 94 Hanover Street ☎ 0131 225 2131 🕔 Mon–Sat 8AM–10:30PM (Sundays during Festival) 🚌 23, 27, 48, 49

Iggs (££)

A popular award-winning Old Town restaurant that combines a Spanish *tapas* bar at lunch time with top-quality organic Scottish cuisine at night, specialising in seafood and beef.

✉ 15 Jeffrey Street ☎ 0131 557 8184 🕔 Mon–Sat 12–2:30, 6–10:30 🚌 1, 3, 6, 7

Iguana (££)

A fashionable café-bar that serves an intriguing selection of international cuisine; popular with students from nearby Edinburgh University, and with a friendly relaxed atmosphere.

✉ 41 Lothian Street ☎ 0131 220 4288 🕔 Daily 9AM–1AM. 🚌 2, 41

Indian Cavalry Club (££)

A classy New-Wave Indian restaurant in the West End, serving an outstanding range of authentic dishes; décor includes a tented roof in the downstairs section.

✉ 3 Atholl Place ☎ 0131 228

3282 🕔 Daily 12–2, 5:30–11:30 🚌 2, 12, 16

Jacksons (££)

In a basement off the Royal Mile, very much aimed at the tourist trade but none the worse for that, serving up the full range of Scottish specialities and a good selection of whiskies, and full of atmosphere.

✉ 209 High Street ☎ 0131 225 1793 🕔 Daily 12–2:30, 6–10:30 🚌 1, 6, 34, 35

Kalpna (£)

This well-established Southside Indian restaurant serves a wide range of vegetarian dishes, subtly blending fresh spices into authentic Gujerati flavours.

✉ 2–3 St Patrick's Square ☎ 0131 667 9890 🕔 Mon–Fri 12–2, 5:30–11; Sat 5:30–11 🚌 3, 5, 7, 8

Kweilin (££)

This relaxed and popular New Town restaurant, serving highest-quality Cantonese cuisine, is an established favourite for Edinburgh diners, so booking is advisable.

✉ 19–21 Dundas Street ☎ 0131 557 1875 🕔 Tue–Sat 12–10:30; Sun 5–10:30 🚌 23, 27

Le Sept (££)

This attractive and lively bistro, tucked off the Royal Mile, specialises in *crêpes* with a wide range of delicious fillings. Both vegetarians and steak eaters are catered for.

✉ 7 Old Fishmarket Close ☎ 0131 225 5428 🕔 Mon–Thu 12–2:15, 6–10; Fri 12:30–11; Sat 12–10:30; Sun 12–9:30 🚌 1, 6

Loon Fung (££)

Popular Canonmills restaurant that has earned its well-founded reputation by serving a wide range of Cantonese specialities, incorporating fish, meat and vegetarian dishes, in a

friendly atmosphere.

✉ **2 Warriston Place** ☎ **0131 556 1781** 🕐 **Mon–Thu 12–11:30; Fri 12–12:30; Sat 2–12:30; Sun 2–11:30** 🚌 **8A, 9A, 23, 27, 37**

Maison Hector (££)

This stylish Stockbridge bistro attracts a lively clientele that comes to enjoy light meals or a wider selection of Scottish and Continental cuisine, served in an agreeably relaxed atmosphere.

✉ **47-49 Deanhaugh Street** ☎ **0131 332 5328** 🕐 **Mon–Wed 11AM–12PM; Thu and Fri 11AM–1AM; Sat 10:30AM–1AM; Sun 10:30AM–12AM** 🚌 **20, 28**

Mamma's (£)

Long-established Grassmarket pizza parlour, with an impressive and delicious range of over 40 toppings, excellent starters and desserts, served by friendly staff in lively informal surroundings.

✉ **30 The Grassmarket** ☎ **0131 225 6464** 🕐 **Sun–Thu 12–11; Fri and Sat 12–12** 🚌 **2, 12**

Marrakech (££)

This basement New Town restaurant serves a good selection of authentic Moroccan cuisine in a friendly atmosphere, with couscous and lamb proving popular; take your own wine, if required.

✉ **30 London Street** ☎ **0131 556 4444** 🕐 **Daily 6–9:30** 🚌 **8, 9, 13**

Martins (£££)

Imaginative use of the best of naturally produced Scottish produce has led to a number of awards for this well-established restaurant, hidden away in a New Town back alley. No smoking, and booking advisable.

✉ **70 Rose Street, North Lane** ☎ **0131 225 3106** 🕐 **Tue–Fri 12–2, 7–10; Sat 7–10** 🚌 **2, 3, 24, 39**

Montpelier's (££)

Stylish Bruntsfield bistro open all day for tempting breakfasts, international lunch and dinner dishes and speciality cocktails.

✉ **159–161 Bruntsfield Place** ☎ **0131 229 3115** 🕐 **Daily 9AM–1AM** 🚌 **11, 15, 16**

Mussel Inn (££)

Shellfish and other seafoods are brought directly to this attractive restaurant in the heart of the New Town, ensuring the freshest of mussels, scallops and other succulent fish.

✉ **61–65 Rose Street** ☎ **0131 225 5979** 🕐 **Daily 12–10** 🚌 **2, 3, 24, 39**

New Edinburgh Rendezvous (££)

Edinburgh's longest-established Chinese restaurant is still providing Peking cuisine to a high standard in the West End; it also offers an imaginative selection of set menus.

✉ **10a Queensferry Street** ☎ **0131 225 2023** 🕐 **Mon–Sat 12–2, 5:30–11; Sun 1–11** 🚌 **19, 34, 35**

New York Steam Packet (£)

Themed on a ship's cabin, this inconspicuous New Town restaurant offers steaks, burgers and vegetarian dishes, with tasty starters; bring your own wine, if required.

✉ **31 Rose Street,, North Lane** ☎ **0131 220 4825** 🕐 **Daily 6–11** 🚌 **17, 39**

Number One (£££)

Classy restaurant in the Balmoral Hotel (► 100), offering luxury cooking at luxury prices – quality ingredients, attentive service and superb wine list.

✉ **1 Princes Street** ☎ **0131 557 6727** 🕐 **Mon–Thu 12–2, 7–10; Fri 12–2, 7–10:30; Sat 7–10:30; Sun 7–10** 🚌 **3, 11, 21, 44**

The Fish Supper

Don't miss the chance to try a local fish and chip shop; Edinburgh fish suppers (always a 'supper' even if eaten at lunch time) are excellent, as are the other offerings which will include haggis, pies and black and white pudding, all deep-fried in batter. Edinburgh suppers are normally liberally dowsed with brown sauce; if you want vinegar, ask for it specifically.

What to Wear in Edinburgh

Clothes-wise, no matter what time of year you visit, be prepared for anything as Edinburgh's weather can change seemingly in the wink of an eye. Wear layers which you can shed and replace, always have a waterproof, and in winter make sure your outer layers are windproof; Edinburgh winds can have a knife-edge. Locals' outfits range from chic and fashionable to designed-for-comfort, so you needn't worry about sartorial elegance.

Pancho Villas (££)

This lively Mexican restaurant is a very popular party venue, located in the Royal Mile. It offers authentic national dishes and an excellent choice of vegetarian meals.

✉ 240 Canongate ☎ 0131 557 4416 🕐 Mon–Thu 12–2:30, 6–10:30; Fri 12–10:30; Sat 12–11; Sun 6–10:30 (summer 12–10:30); Jul, Aug daily 12–11 🚌 1, 6

Petit Paris (££)

A popular Grassmarket restaurant with a friendly atmosphere serving a well-balanced range of authentic French cuisine in a straight-forward manner. There are both traditional dishes and delicious *crêpes*; take your own wine if required.

✉ 38–40 Grassmarket ☎ 0131 226 2442 🕐 Daily 12–3, 5:30–11 🚌 2, 12

Point Restaurant (££)

The spacious, modern décor of this hotel restaurant is an added incentive to sample the culinary treats on offer; the imaginative set menu is excellent value, featuring Scottish specialities with a twist and some very serious puddings.

✉ 34 Bread Street ☎ 0131 221 5555 🕐 Mon–Wed 12–2, 6–9:30; Thu–Sat 12–2, 6–10:30. Closed Sun 🚌 11, 15, 23

Siam Erawan (££)

This Thai restaurant is located in a small New Town cellar, with a lively atmosphere and an authentic range of aromatic delicacies; this is a very popular eatery, so booking is advisable.

✉ 48 Howe Street ☎ 0131 226 3675 🕐 Mon–Sat 12–2:30, 6–11; Sun 6–10:30 🚌 20, 28, 80

Skippers (££)

Skippers has long been recognised as one of Leith's leading seafood bistros. It has a great waterside location where you'll enjoy a wide selection of delicious fish specialities. Again, you are advised to book in advance.

✉ 1a Dock Place, Leith ☎ 0131 554 1018 🕐 Mon–Sat 12:30–2, 7–10 🚌 10A, 16, 22A, 32, 52

Stac Polly (££)

Concentrating on the innovative use of traditional Scottish cuisine, this New Town restaurant, with its stone walls and tartan decoration, serves a range of typical Scottish dishes. Popular with tourists and locals.

✉ 29-33 Dublin Street ☎ 0131 556 2231 🕐 Mon–Sat 12–2, 6–10; Sat and Sun 6–10 🚌 8, 9, 13

Tampopo (££)

Tiny New Town Japanese noodle bar that specialises in take-aways, but with a few stools for in-house eating. Delicacies ranging from sushi to exquisite *bento* meals make it Edinburgh's finest Japanese establishment.

✉ 25a Thistle Street ☎ 0131 220 5254 🕐 Mon 12–3; Tue–Sat 12–3, 6–9 🚌 23, 27

Tapas Olé (££)

A relaxed and friendly Canonmills restaurant that offers a wide range of delicious Spanish *tapas*; choose a selection for a hearty meal.

✉ 10 Eyre Place ☎ 0131 556 2754 🕐 Daily 12–11 🚌 8, 9, 23, 27

Tapas Tree (££)

Popular Spanish restaurant off Broughton Street offering an impressive choice of authentic meat, fish and vegetarian *tapas* in a buzzing atmosphere, with a fine selection of Spanish beers and wines; booking advised.

✉ **1 Forth Street** ☎ **0131 556 7118** 🕐 **Daily 12–11PM** 🚌 **8, 9, 19, 39**

36 (£££)

In the basement of the Howard Hotel in the New Town (▶ 101) can be found some of Edinburgh's finest food, with an impressive selection of Scottish and international dishes served in opulent surroundings.

✉ **36 Great King Street** ☎ **0131 556 3638** 🕐 **Sun–Fri 12–2, 7–10; Sat 7–10** 🚌 **13, 23, 27, 47**

Tower (££)

The modern interior of this stylish restaurant above the Museum of Scotland, with superb views over Old Town to the castle, provides a pleasant setting for dining out with a wide choice of eclectic dishes.

✉ **Museum of Scotland, Chambers Street** ☎ **0131 225 3003** 🕐 **Mon–Sat 10AM–11PM; Sun 12–11** 🚌 **41, 42, 45**

Vintners Rooms (£££)

Magnificently housed in two rooms of a former Leith warehouse, this restaurant is *the* place to enjoy the finest French provincial cooking, using many of Scotland's finest ingredients, with an extensive wine list; no smoking.

✉ **The Vaults, 87 Giles Street** ☎ **0131 554 6767** 🕐 **Mon–Sat 12–2, 7–10:30** 🚌 **1, 6, 7, 10**

Viva Mexico (££)

This well-established and popular Old Town Mexican restaurant offers a good choice of authentic spicy dishes, served in a relaxed and friendly atmosphere.

✉ **41 Cockburn Street** ☎ **0131 226 5145** 🕐 **Mon–Sat 12–2:30, 6:30–10:30; Sun 6:30–10** 🚌 **1, 6, 30**

Waterfront (££)

This comfortably relaxed restaurant is found by the waterfront in Leith, where a good range of imaginative and well-prepared fish, meat and vegetarian dishes is served in a vine-clad conservatory.

✉ **1c Dock Place, Leith** ☎ **0131 554 7427** 🕐 **Mon–Thu 12–11; Fri and Sat 12–12; Sun 12:30–10:30** 🚌 **10A ,16, 22A, 32, 52**

Winter Glen (£££)

A classy New Town basement restaurant; the emphasis is on Scottish cooking with a twist. The desserts are particularly mouth-watering and the service is friendly.

✉ **3 Dundas Street** ☎ **0131 477 7060** 🕐 **Mon–Thu 12–2, 6–10; Fri and Sat 12–2, 6–10:30** 🚌 **19, 23, 27**

Witchery by the Castle (£££)

Two candlelit dining rooms close to the castle comprise one of Edinburgh's best restaurants, where you can sample an interesting range of Scottish cuisine complemented by wine from the huge list, to ensure a special meal out.

✉ **352 Castlehill** ☎ **0131 225 5613** 🕐 **Daily 12–4, 5:30–11:30** 🚌 **1, 6, 34, 35**

Quick Lunches

Lunch often seems a waste of time if you're packing in the sightseeing, and Edinburgh has plenty of quick options. The entire city is liberally sprinkled with excellent takeaway sandwich bars, though many have a few tables for sit-down eating. You'll find food courts in shopping malls, while many museums and attractions have their own restaurants and cafés.

Outside Edinburgh

High Tea

If you're exploring outside Edinburgh, you'll have the chance to sample high tea, still very much a Scots institution. This meal, eaten between 5 and 6:30 or so, comprises a main course, which can be anything from a groaning plate of fried goodies to a fresh salmon salad, followed by cakes, scones and biscuits, all washed down with tea. Home-baking often features in country places, giving you a chance to try specialities such as treacle and potato scones, pancakes eaten with butter and jam, and calorie-laden fruit cake, shortbread and meringues.

Anstruther

The Cellar Restaurant (££)

Diners love this fine seafood restaurant, housed in a converted cooperage close to Anstruther harbour. Only the very best of local produce is used; reservations essential.

✉ 24 East Green ☎ 01333 310378 🕐 Wed–Sat 12:30–1:30; Tue–Sat 7–9:30; May–Sep also open Mon PM

Glasgow

Axiom (££)

Classy modern restaurant beside the Clyde, bright and minimalist in design, serving an enormous range of quality dishes at all price ranges and quantities as desired.

✉ Lancefield Quay, 154 Hydepark Street ☎ 0141 221 2822 🕐 Mon–Sat 12–11

Babbity Bowster (£)

A combination of traditional pub and Continental café, this lively, stylish 18th-century town house offers traditional Scottish fare, light meals and more substantial French dishes in a unique atmosphere.

✉ 16–18 Blackfriars ☎ 0141 552 5055 🕐 Mon–Sat 8AM–12PM; Sun 9AM–12PM

City Merchant (££)

This family-run central rest-aurant specialises in Scottish produce, with superb fish and seafood, beef and lamb dishes providing good value for money.

✉ 97–99 Candleriggs ☎ 0141 553 1577 🕐 Mon–Sat 12–11; Sun 5–11

One Devonshire Gardens (£££)

West End Michelin-star restaurant serving only the very finest produce in luxurious surroundings, with emphasis on game, meat, fish and seafood dishes, and wicked desserts.

✉ 1 Devonshire Gardens ☎ 0141 339 2001 🕐 Sun–Fri 12–2, 7:15–9:45; Sat 7:15–9:45

The Ubiquitous Chip (££)

A Glasgow institution, this established West End restaurant serves the best of Scottish cuisine in stylish surroundings, with plenty of game and venison dishes, but no chips.

✉ 12 Ashton Lane, Hillhead ☎ 0141 334 5007 🕐 Mon–Sat 12–2:30, 5:30–11; Sun 12:30–2:30, 6:30–11

Vegville (£)

Popular and cosy vegetarian restaurant. Its imaginative range of dishes displays culinary influences from all over the world; cheap and friendly.

✉ 93 St George's Road ☎ 0141 572 1160 🕐 Mon–Sat 10–1AM; Sun 12:30–11

Haddington

Waterside (£)

This award-winning restaurant and bistro is attractively sited beside the River Tyne and historic St Mary's Church, and offers fine bar luncheons and suppers, as well as more substantial restaurant meals.

✉ 1–5 Waterside, Nungate ☎ 01620 825674 🕐 Daily 12–2, 6:30–10

Innerleithen

Traquair Arms Hotel (££)

Exceptional 19th-century country inn, with warm friendly welcome and choice of well-prepared local dishes in three dining areas. It has a fine wine list and a variety of real ales; reservations required for dinner.

✉ Traquair Road ☎ 01896 830229 🕓 Daily 12–3; 7–9

Kilmahog
The Lade Inn (££)

This attractive pub, situated in beautiful wooded surroundings, serves a selection of excellent freshly made food, including venison, in its two dining rooms; the terraced garden sometimes offers summer barbecues.

✉ Trossachs Road, Kilmahog, by Callander ☎ 01877 330152 🕓 Daily 12–2:30 (3:15 Sun), 5:30–9

Linlithgow
The Four Marys (£)

Friendly pub and restaurant themed on the serving-women of the ill-fated Mary, Queen of Scots, with excellent lunches and evening meals served daily, and a wide range of real ales.

✉ 65 High Street ☎ 01506 842171 🕓 Mon–Sat 12–2:30, 5:30–8:30; Sun 12:30–2:30

Melrose
Marmions (£)

Located close to historic Melrose Abbey, this French-style *brasserie* specialises in a range of dishes based on local ingredients, served in the elegant setting of an oak-panelled gallery.

✉ Buccleuch Street ☎ 01896 822245 🕓 Mon–Sat 9AM–12PM

Peat Inn
The Peat Inn (£££)

This award-winning former coaching inn has built an excellent reputation for serving the very best of freshest produce from the countryside and the sea, with a fine wine list and a friendly, yet formal, atmosphere.

✉ Peat Inn, Cupar ☎ 01334 840206 🕓 Tue–Sat set lunch at 1, 7–9:30

St Andrews
The Grange Inn (££)

A very attractive old inn on a hillside just over a kilometre (1 mile) to the south of the town, with three dining areas offering excellent light lunches and gourmet dinners in delightful surroundings.

✉ Grange Road ☎ 01334 472 670 🕓 Wed–Sun 12–2; 7–9:30

The Vine Leaf (££)

A popular centrally-situated restaurant that specialises in game, seafood and gourmet vegetarian dishes served in attractive surroundings, with an extensive wine list; note that this is a smoke-free zone.

✉ 131 South Street ☎ 01334 477497 🕓 Tue–Sat 7–9:30

St Boswells
Buccleuch Arms (£)

Friendly family-run hotel, serving good-quality local produce in attractive surroundings, with a choice of bar meals or more formal fare served throughout the day.

✉ The Green ☎ 01835 822 243 🕓 Daily 12–2:30, 6:30–9:30

St Monans
Ichthus (££)

This excellent non-smoking seafood restaurant, with fine views over the harbour and Forth Estuary, uses local produce to great effect in a friendly atmosphere, and also offers the option of *alfresco* dining.

✉ 16 West End ☎ 01333 730 327 🕓 Daily 12–2:30, 6:30–9:30

Stirling
The River House (£)

This friendly restaurant boasts a fine waterside location and excellent views to the castle and Wallace Monument, and serves delicious freshly prepared food at reasonable prices.

✉ Castle Business Park, Craigforth ☎ 01786 465577 🕓 Daily 12–2:30, 6:30–9:30

When to Eat

Outside Edinburgh, relatively few restaurants serve dinner much after 9:30, a point worth bearing in mind if you're on the road. Lunch service starts around 12:30 and often finishes by 2, though an increasing number of establishments in tourist areas will have something simple on the go throughout the day.

Edinburgh

Prices

The price indications below are per person with breakfast included:

£ = budget (£25–£35)
££ = moderate (£35–£65)
£££ = expensive (over £65)

Note that rooms in de-luxe hotels such as the Balmoral and the Caledonian may cost well over £100 per person. Bed and breakfast accommodation normally ranges from £18 to £25 per person including breakfast.

A-Haven Town House (££)

This very welcoming family-run town house on the north side of the city has refurbished many of its well-equipped rooms, making it a comfortable place to stay.
✉ 180 Ferry Road ☎ 0131 554 6559; fax 0131 554 5252
🕐 All year 🚌 1, 6

Ailsa Craig (£)

You can enjoy the Georgian splendours of the Royal Terrace by staying in this comfortable and reasonably priced hotel, only 10 minutes' walk from Waverley Station.
✉ 24 Royal Terrace ☎ 0131 556 1022; fax 0131 556 6055
🕐 All year 🚌 12, 13, 16

Apex International (££)

This excellent-value city-centre hotel offers good, international-standard accom-modation in family-size en-suite rooms, with the bonus of a rooftop restaurant giving fine views to the castle.
✉ 31–5 Grassmarket ☎ 0131 300 3456; fax 0131 220 5345 🕐 All year 🚌 2, 12

Balmoral (£££)

This luxury hotel dominates the east end of Princes Street. Its Edwardian splendours include superb accommodation, a gourmet restaurant (► 95), bars and swimming pool, and the standard of service you would expect from an establishment of this calibre.
✉ 1 Princes Street ☎ 0131 556 2414; fax 0131 557 3747
🕐 All year ☎ 3, 11, 21, 44

Bank (££)

This small, distinctive and privately owned hotel in one of the Royal Mile's landmark buildings will appeal to visitors looking for a memorable Scottish experience.
✉ 1 South Bridge ☎ 0131 556 9043; fax 0131 558 1362
🕐 All year 🚌 1, 6

Bruntsfield (££)

This large Victorian town house, just over a kilometre (1 mile) south of Princes Street, has good views over Bruntsfield Links and offers good service and a spacious conservatory-style restaurant.
✉ 69 Bruntsfield Place
☎ 0131 229 1393; fax 0131 229 5634 🕐 All year 🚌 11, 15, 23, 37

Caledonian (£££)

Edinburgh's most famous hotel stands at the west end of Princes Street; the splendours of its interior live up to its ornate exterior, and you'll find the level of comfort, service and facilities associated with a 5-star hotel.
✉ Princes Street ☎ 0131 459 9988; fax 0131 225 6632 🕐 All year 🚌 11, 15, 17

Crowne Plaza (£££)

This big, stylish hotel, with a full range of international-class facilities, is housed in a mock-medieval turreted building right at the heart of the Royal Mile.
✉ 80 High Street , Royal Mile ☎ 0131 557 9797; fax 0131 557 9789 🕐 All year 🚌 1, 6

Dunstane House (£)

This fine Victorian mansion, close to Haymarket Station, offers friendly service, well-equipped rooms, and a residents' bar, all adding up to good value and comfortable surroundings.

✉ 4 West Coates, Haymarket ☎ 0131 337 6169; fax 0131 337 6169 🕐 All year 🚌 2, 12, 16, 18

Galloway Guest House (£)
This family-run Stockbridge guest house is housed in a restored Victorian town house within walking distance of the city centre; excellent value for money.
✉ 22 Dean Park Crescent ☎ 0131 332 3672; fax 0131 332 3672 🕐 All year 🚌 34, 35

Hotel Ibis (££)
This new modern city centre hotel (part of an international chain) almost on the Royal Mile, offers good-value, if bland, accommodation and has a restaurant.
✉ 6 Hunter Square ☎ 0131 240 7000; fax 0131 240 7007 🕐 All year 🚌 3, 7, 8

Howard (£££)
This sophisticated hotel, formed from three connected 18th-century New Town houses, has lovely rooms, elegant public areas, an outstanding restaurant (► 97) and all the facilities you'd expect.
✉ 34 Great King Street ☎ 0131 557 3500; fax 0131 557 6515 🕐 All year 🚌 13, 23, 27, 47

Maitland (££)
This hotel near the west end of Princes Street has been refurbished and now provides a comfortable base right in the city centre.
✉ 25–33 Shandwick Place ☎ 0131 229 1467; fax 0131 229 7549 🕐 All year 🚌 3, 4, 12, 21

Malmaison (£££)
An old seaman's mission at Leith houses this classic contemporary hotel, deservedly popular for its great waterfront views, and with a good art nouveau-style French *brasserie*.

✉ 1 Tower Place ☎ 0131 468 5000/5003; fax 0131 468 5002 🕐 All year 🚌 1, 6, 10A, 32, 52

Rothesay Hotel (£)
A quiet hotel in a residential area close to St Mary's Cathedral, with pleasant en-suite bedrooms and friendly service. Ideal if you're looking for a peaceful location.
✉ 8 Rothesay Place ☎ 0131 225 4125; fax 0131 220 4350 🕐 All year 🚌 13

Royal Circus Hotel (££)
Situated in one of the New Town's most elegant architectural ensembles, this hotel offers friendly service in a location within easy reach of the city centre.
✉ 19–21 Royal Circus ☎ 0131 220 5000; fax 0131 220 2020 🕐 All year 🚌 13, 20, 28

Stuart House (£)
A non-smoking hotel in a traditional Georgian town house north of the city centre, providing comfortable guest-house accommodation in good-sized, chintzy bedrooms.
✉ 12 East Claremont Street ☎ 0131 557 9030; fax 0131 557 0563 🕐 All year 🚌 8, 9, 34

Town House (£)
A small, friendly Victorian town house, about 15 minutes' walk from Princes Street. The rooms are comfortable, and a there is a non-smoking policy.
✉ 65 Gilmore Place ☎ 0131 229 1985 🕐 All year 🚌 10, 27

Travel Inn (£)
A big, basic budget hotel around 10 minutes' walk from Princes Street. Its two-double-bed rooms are ideal for families, and there's a restaurant, but few other services.
✉ 1 Morrison Street Link, Haymarket ☎ 0131 228 9819; fax 0131 228 9836 🕐 All year 🚌 2, 12, 16, 18

Accommodation Grading
The Scottish Tourist Board operates a grading system for every type of accommodation available in Scotland. Hotels, guest houses, bed-and-breakfast establishments and other types of tourist accommodation are inspected annually and awarded anything from 1 to 5 stars. Stars are awarded on the basis of the facilities offered and are displayed on a blue plaque with a thistle symbol outside the property.

Outside Edinburgh

Self-catering

If you're planning to stay outside Edinburgh and travel in daily to enjoy the city, it's worth considering renting self-catering accommodation. You could find yourself staying in anything from an idyllic cottage to the wing of a castle. Even in Edinburgh itself, there are self-catering options on offer. The Edinburgh and Lothians Tourist Board publishes full details of self-catering options in its annual accommodation guide and also provides a booking service.

Anstruther

Smugglers Inn (£)

This historic roadside inn, overlooking the harbour, retains its original character and offerss a high level of service and cuisine.

✉ High Street ☎ 01333 310506; fax 01333 312706 🕐 All year

Crail

Balcomie Links Hotel (£)

A friendly family-run hotel close to the golf course on the east edge of town; sea views and pleasant rooms go hand in hand with tasty home cooking, a good-value choice.

✉ Balcomie Road ☎ 01333 450237; fax 01333 450540 🕐 All year

Dirleton

Open Arms Hotel (££)

This old-established classy country inn is attractively situated close to the village green and castle, and offers a high degree of comfort and excellent food from an imaginative menu.

✉ Dirleton ☎ 01620 850241; fax 01620 850570 🕐 All year

Freuchie

Lomond Hills Hotel (££)

This former coaching inn in the centre of the village has been extended but still retains much of its original character. Pretty rooms, Scottish and French cuisine, and indoor leisure centre with heated swimming pool.

✉ Lomond Road ☎ 01337 857329; fax 01337 857329 🕐 All year

Glasgow

Brunswick Merchant City Hotel (££)

A modern stylish hotel in a building that offers plenty of architectural interest. Completed in 1995, it offers good-value accommodation and high-quality service, together with an excellent restaurant.

✉ 106–108 Brunswick Street ☎ 0141 552 0001; fax 0141 552 1551 🕐 All year 🚍 66 A/B/C

Copthorne (£££)

Centrally situated on the north side of George Square, this large and impressive hotel has the grandest accommodation in the city, with restaurant and bar to match.

✉ 40 George Square ☎ 0141 332 6711; fax 0141 332 4264 🕐 All year 🚇 Buchanan Street; Queen Street

Town House (£)

Two converted Edwardian houses in an elegant crescent offer excellent budget accommodation, mostly en suite, friendly attentive service and a basement dining room.

✉ 21 Royal Crescent ☎ 0141 332 9009; fax 0141 353 9604 🕐 All year 🚍 42, 57(A)

Gullane

Greywalls Hotel (£££)

A luxurious hotel in a wonderful, Lutyens-designed Edwardian mansion, set in a walled garden overlooking Muirfield Golf Course

✉ Muirfield, Gullane ☎ 01620 842 144; fax 01620 842 241 🕐 All year

Lower Largo

Crusoe Hotel (££)

With magnificent views across Largo Bay, this comfortable hotel has an excellent restaurant and bars, themed around Alexander Selkirk, the local whose adventures were immortalised in Daniel Defoe's novel *Robinson Crusoe*.

✉ **The Harbour, Lower Largo** ☎ 01333 320759; fax 01333 320865 🎨 All year

Melrose

Burts Hotel (££)

This friendly family-run townhouse hotel, built in 1722, with comfortable well-appointed rooms, has gained a well-earned reputation for providing first-class cuisine.

✉ **Market Square** ☎ 01896 822285; fax 01896 822870 🎨 All year

Peebles

Castle Venlaw Hotel (££)

A family-run hotel in an imposing 18th-century castle with lovely countryside views towards Peebles, where you'll find pretty public rooms, good food and friendly staff.

✉ **Edinburgh Road** ☎ 01721 720384; fax 01721 724066 🎨 All year

Roslin

Roslin Glen Hotel (££)

Comfortable and friendly hotel 11km (7 miles) south of Edinburgh, well placed for the chapel (➤ 85) and Roslin Castle, with personal service and a good restaurant.

✉ **2 Penicuik Road** ☎ 0131 440 2029; fax 0131 440 2229 🎨 All year

St Andrews

Hazelbank Hotel (££)

This centrally situated hotel, with fine views over St Andrews Bay, and just a few minutes' walk from the Old Course, is a good bet for golfers and tourists alike.

✉ **28 The Scores** ☎ 01334 472466; fax 01334 472466 🎨 All year

Number Ten (£)

This compact and cosy Edwardian guest house offers good-value accommodation in the centre of town, with comfortable rooms and full facilities.

✉ **10 Hope Street** ☎ 01334 474 601; fax 01334 474 601 🎨 Mar–Nov

Old Course Hotel (£££)

St Andrews' luxury hotel, unattractive from outside, is nevertheless bright and comfortable inside with sweeping views of the Old Course, high standards of service and comfort and good facilities.

✉ **Golf Resort and Spa, St Andrews** ☎ 01334 474 371; fax 1334 477 668 🎨 All year

St Boswells

Dryburgh Abbey Hotel (££)

An attractive country hotel romantically situated in fine 'policies' (parklands) close to the Abbey beside the River Tweed. As well as the usual amenities it has the bonus of an indoor swimming pool.

✉ **Dryburgh Abbey** ☎ 01835 822 261; fax 01835 823945 🎨 All year

Scone

Murrayshall Country House Hotel (££)

A pleasantly situated hotel right next to a golf course, set in the rolling countryside north of Perth. The hotel is well-equipped and has a friendly atmosphere and good food.

✉ **Scone, Perth** ☎ 01738 551171; fax 01738 552595 🎨 All year

The Trossachs

Callander

Roman Camp Hotel (££)

Discerning visitors flock to this turreted and romantic 17th-century country house in wooded grounds beside the River Teith, to enjoy the high standard of comfort and excellent food.

✉ **Callander** ☎ 01877 330003; fax 01877 331533 🎨 All year

Guesthouses, Hotels and B & Bs

Edinburgh has a huge number of both guest houses and small family-run hotels. The essential difference between guest houses and hotels is that the latter will be a little larger, have more rooms with private facilities and will be licensed. If you are looking for something more personal, B&Bs are ideal. They offer a higher standard of comfort and give you the chance to sample some wonderful Scottish breakfasts, complete with home-made porridge, oatcakes and black pudding.

Edinburgh

Edinburgh v Glasgow Shopping

Until recently it was an acknowledged fact that Glasgow had the edge over Edinburgh when it came to shopping, with designer names, huge choice and the type of avant-garde fashion unobtainable in Edinburgh. Things have changed, however, and Edinburgh's shopping scene now rivals its western neighbour. With Harvey Nichols planning its third store outside London in Edinburgh, it seems as if the capital's shopping has caught up definitively.

Books

James Thin

An Edinburgh institution that has been providing a comprehensive range of general and academic books and publications for over 150 years.

✉ **53–59 South Bridge Street**
☎ **0131 556 6743** 🚌 **7, 8, 9, 30**

Clothing and Woollens

Burberrys and the Scotch House

Fashionable trenchcoats and rainwear are on one side of this popular Princes Street store; other has an extensive range of traditional Scottish knitwear, tartan and gifts.

✉ **39–41 Princes Street**
☎ **0131 556 1252** 🚌 **3, 11, 21, 44**

The Cashmere Store

Royal Mile store selling sweaters, cardigans, scarves, dresses and skirts with a serious touch of luxury.

✉ **379 High Street, Royal Mile**
☎ **0131 225 5178** 🚌 **1, 6**

John Dickson and Son

Long-established New Town store stocking high-quality country clothing by all the leading manufacturers, and a full range of fishing and shooting accessories in atmospheric surroundings.

✉ **21 Frederick Street**
☎ **0131 225 4218** 🚌 **13, 20, 28**

Judith Glue

Attractive and unusual knitwear, hand framed on the Orkney Islands, as well as a choice of gifts.

✉ **64 High Street, Royal Mile**
☎ **0131 556 5443** 🚌 **1, 6**

Kinloch Anderson

Every aspect of traditional Highland dress is catered for in this long-established Leith establishment – tartan trousers, jackets and kilt outfits, skirts and accessories. Exhibition on the history of tartan.

✉ **Commercial Street/Dock Street, Leith** ☎ **0131 555 1390**
🚌 **16, 22, 88**

Number Two

Friendly Stockbridge shop stocking a tempting selection of high-quality knitwear, designed and produced in Britain.

✉ **2 St Stephen Place**
☎ **0131 225 6257** 🚌 **20, 28, 34**

Department Stores

Jenners

The world's oldest independent department store, founded in 1838, with six floors selling a range of high-quality goods. There are instore restaurants, an air of old-fashioned courtesy and décor to match.

✉ **48 Princes Street** ☎ **0131 225 2442** 🚌 **3, 11, 21, 44**

Food and Drink

Justerini and Brooks

This notable and spacious New Town emporium has been supplying high-quality wines and malt whiskies for over 250 years, and produces its own well-known blend of the latter.

✉ **45 George Street** ☎ **0131 226 4202** 🚌 **12, 22, 33, 51**

Peckhams

The place to buy MacSween's award-winning haggis, considered to be the best and made for world-wide export, along with a myriad other specialities.

✉ 155–159 Bruntsfield Place
☎ 0131 440 2555 🚌 11, 15, 16, 23

Royal Mile Whiskies
Over 300 whiskies, including some very rare, and Havana cigars, in this traditional shop popular with tourists and Scots alike.

✉ 379 High Street, Royal Mile
☎ 0131 225 3383 🚌 1, 6

Valvona and Crolla
An Edinburgh institution, this long narrow food and wine shop provides the very best of all things Italian.

✉ 19 Elm Row ☎ 0131 556 6066 🚌 2, 7, 10, 14

Jewellery

Hamilton and Inches
Edinburgh's most famous jeweller is elegantly housed in chandelier-hung premises in the New Town, and stocks an extensive selection of expensive antique and modern jewellery.

✉ 87 George Street ☎ 0131 225 4898 🚌 12, 22, 33, 51

Joseph Bonnar
Attractive New Town shop on Thistle Street, renowned for the variety and prices on offer.

✉ 72 Thistle Street ☎ 0131 226 2811 🚌 3, 4, 7

Music, Tapes & CDs

Blackfriars Folk Music Shop
Huge range of folk and traditional Scottish music, traditional instruments and music magazines.

✉ 49 Blackfriars Street
☎ 0131 557 3090 🚌 1, 6

Specialist

Cyberia
Roomy internet café in the New Town, with complete facilities for surfing and e-mail and a useful public e-mail drop box. Licensed bar and refreshments are available.

✉ 88 Hanover Street ☎ 0131 220 4403 🚌 23, 27, 37, 47

Griselda Hill Pottery
Attractive selection of distinctive Wemyss Ware reproductions, with brightly coloured cats and pigs, and other pottery, all hand painted and made by skilled craftspeople, in pleasant shop off the Grassmarket.

✉ 89 West Bow ☎ 0131 226 1479 🚌 1, 28, 40

International Newsagents
This newsagent stocks a wide range of European and American daily papers, as well as a selection of international magazines.

✉ 351 High Street, Royal Mile
☎ 0131 225 4827 🚌 1, 6, 34, 35

Robert Cresser
Every conceivable type of broom and brush has been sold from this individual shop off the Grassmarket for over 125 years, where little seems to have changed since it opened.

✉ 40 Victoria Street ☎ 0131 225 2181 🚌 1, 28, 40

Somerville Playing Cards
The widest range of cards in Europe, both playing and Tarot, with over 2000 designs, stocked in a fascinating shop on the Royal Mile.

✉ 82 Canongate, Royal Mile
☎ 0131 556 5225 🚌 1, 6

Studio One
This West End shop is popular with all ages for its variety of unusual gifts, furnishings and household items in a basement setting.

✉ 10–16 Stafford Street
☎ 0131 226 5812 🚌 2, 3, 12, 21

Valvona and Crolla
Foodies should make a point of heading down the Leith Walk to visit Valvona and Crolla, one of Britain's great food stores. Founded in the 1870s to serve Edinburgh's burgeoning Italian community, the ceiling-high shelves of this long, narrow shop offer a cornucopia of the finest and freshest Italian produce and wines. Mozzarella is trucked in from Naples, Italian-style bread baked daily and coffee is roasted beneath the Parma hams and gaily boxed *panettone* hanging from the roof. Service is cheery and professional, prices are reasonable – what more could you want?

Outside Edinburgh

The Little Streets

Some of Edinburgh's most enticing shops are tucked off the beaten track, many of them in the narrow streets that run parallel with the grand New Town thoroughfares. Rose Street, between Princes and George streets, Thistle Street and Hill Street behind Queen Street, and William Street in the West End are all worth exploring for their attractive shops, restaurants and trendy bars and cafés.

Cupar

Scottish Deer Centre

The Scottish Deer centre offers the best of courtyard shopping for traditional Scottish knitwear, food and whisky, as well as falconry, deer and adventure play parks.

✉ **Bow-of-Fife, by Cupar** ☎ **01337 810391**

Galashiels

Scottish Cashmere and Wool Centre

This mill has an excellent range of the finest knitwear, tweeds and tartan woven from cashmere, mohair and lambswool, plus conducted tours and an interesting museum of weaving.

✉ **Waverley Mill, Huddersfield Street** ☎ **01896 752091**

Glasgow

The Barras

A large covered and open market that has become a Glaswegian institution, with over 1,000 traders selling every imaginable item. Operates weekends only (9–5), and has a great atmosphere.

✉ **244 Gallowgate** ☎ **0141 552 7258**

Italian Centre

At the northern edge of Merchant City, this group of shops stocks the best of all things Italian, particularly fashion items, in a stylish mall.

✉ **7 John Street** ☎ **0141 552 6368**

Princes Square

City-centre mecca for shoppers seeking the latest fashions and quality goods in a glass-domed listed building, with six floors of luxury shops and restaurants.

✉ **48 Buchanan Street** ☎ **0141 221 0324**

St Enoch Centre

The largest glass-roofed construction in Europe houses a wide range of the familiar high-street stores, as well as speciality outlets. There is a large car park, and an ice rink.

✉ **55 St Enoch Sqare** ☎ **0141 204 3900**

Slater Menswear

The largest store in the world specialising in men's suits and accessories, with a vast selection of top designs and labels at discount prices.

✉ **165 Howard Street** ☎ **0141 552 7171**

Kelty

The Butterchurn

The best of Scottish food and handmade crafts is available in the courtyard of a traditional farm steading, with a diverse choice of cheeses, wines, whiskies and seafood.

✉ **Cocklaw Mains Farm, Kelty** ☎ **01383 830 169**

Penicuik

The Edinburgh Crystal Visitor Centre

The centre has the world's largest selection of Edinburgh crystal. You can tour the factory and see the video and exhibition before hitting the factory shop with its range of items at discounted prices.

✉ **Eastfield, Penicuik** ☎ **01968 675128**

Pittenweem

Fishermans Mutual Association

Wonderful store stocking a vast range of ships' chandlery, workwear and all things nautical in harbourside position, run by the fishermen of Pittenweem.

✉ **23 East Shore** ☎ **01333 311263**

St Andrews

Auchterlonies of St Andrews

A selection of quality golf equipment from leading manufacturers, close to the final hole of the Old Course, with a wide range of golfing accessories and memorabilia.

✉ **2 Golf Place** ☎ **01334 473253**

David Low Sports

Long-established and well-respected supplier of all things to do with golf, this friendly shop close to the Old Course can offer a complete service and advice for the golfing visitor.

✉ **6 Golf Place** ☎ **01334 473253**

Fisher and Donaldson

Spectacular display of mouth-watering delights at this speciality baker and confectioner in the centre of town, with hand-made chocolates, shortbread and patisserie.

✉ **Church Street** ☎ **01334 472201**

B Jannetta

Some of the finest ice-cream to be found in Scotland, with over 50 varieties and delicious sundaes in this family-run parlour close to the cathedral.

✉ **31 South Street** ☎ **01334 473285**

St Andrews Woollen Mill

A huge selection of knitwear at good prices in an apparently chaotic shop overlooking Old Course, with cashmere, Harris tweed and golfing accessories.

✉ **The Golf Links** ☎ **01334 472366**

Upper Largo

Scotland's Larder

A centre of excellence for the best in Scottish foods, this shop sells memorable delicacies and offers cookery demonstrations, exhibitions and a restaurant.

✉ **Buckthorns, Upper Largo**
☎ **01333 360414**

The Trossachs

Aberfoyle

The Scottish Wool Centre

More than a mere shop, the Centre also offers demonstrations of spinning and weaving, and a live show tracing the history of sheep in Scotland.

✉ **Off Main Street** ☎ **01887 382850**

Kilmahog

Trossachs Woollen Mill

This active woollen mill to the north of Callender stocks a fascinating selection of Scottish knitwear and clothing, tartans, rugs and gifts; visitors enjoy the demonstrations of skilled weaving techniques.

✉ **Kilmahog, by Callendar** ☎ **01887 330178**

Woollens, Cashmere and Tweed

Scottish woollen goods are exported world-wide, so you may wonder if it's worth buying them in Scotland. If you're looking for something of the highest quality at a good price, the answer is 'yes'; with a plethora of factory outlets, prices are keen, particularly for cashmere. Equally, you'll find more-than-adequate knitwear at knock-down prices in the factory shops. Knitters can find a huge range of yarns, unequalled south of the border. High-fashion fans though, are unlikely to find anything at the forefront of design in the mill outlets.

Edinburgh

Help with your Kids

The Edinburgh and Lothians Tourist Board (➤ 118) will send you advance information on children's events and activities, as well as recommending child-friendly accommodation. *Edinburgh for Under Fives*, available from local bookshops, is a useful publication. Baby-sitting can be arranged by the top hotels or contact Edinburgh Crèche Co-op (0131 553 2116), who can organise a baby-sitter or even take the children off your hands for the day.

Brass Rubbing Centre

Children of all ages can try their hand at rubbing brasses at the centre's large collection of replica brasses.
✉ Trinity Apse, Chalmers Close, off Royal Mile ☎ 0131 556 4364 ⏰ Mon–Sat 10–5; Sun during Festival 12–5 🚌 1, 6, 34, 35

Butterfly and Insect World

Colourful and spectacular butterflies together with fascinating and remarkable insects, all in an exotic rainforest habitat. Regular mini-beast handlings.
✉ Dobbies Garden World, Lasswade ☎ 0131 663 4932 ⏰ Apr–Oct 9:30–5:30; Nov–Mar 10–5 🚌 3, 80, 80A

Dalkeith Country Park

Landscaped parklands with waymarked walks through fine woodlands. There's a variety of attractive livestock, and an exciting Woodland Adventure area, with aerial ropeways, giant slides and high-level walkways.
✉ Dalkeith Country Park, Dalkeith ☎ 0131 654 1666 ⏰ Apr–Oct daily 10–6 🚌 3

Edinburgh Canal Centre

This picturesque canalside centre, with its playgrounds and summer sightseeing cruises (Apr–Sep), makes an ideal day out for children.
✉ The Bridge Inn, 27 Baird Road, Ratho ☎ 0131 333 1320 ⏰ Mon–Thu 12–11; Fri–Sat 12–12PM; Sun 12:30–11

Edinburgh Zoo

This is one of Europe's finest wildlife parks, in a spacious hillside setting, and has over 1,000 animals from all over the world; it is particularly popular with children, with a charming daily parade of penguins in summer.
✉ Murrayfield ☎ 0131 334 9171 ⏰ Apr–Sep daily 9–6; Oct, Nov, Mar daily 9–5:30; Jan, Feb daily 9–4:30 🚌 2, 12, 36

Fat Sam's

This is a very children-friendly diner with a lively atmosphere and welcoming staff off the Lothian Road, where grown-ups will have a good time as well.
✉ 56 Fountainbridge ☎ 0131 228 3111 ⏰ Mon–Thu, Sun 12–10; Fri, Sat 12–11 🚌 1, 2, 6, 12

Gorgie City Farm

An ideal spot for the kids to let off steam in informal surroundings, with a wide range of favourite farmyard animals and a playground, and good eating arrangements.
✉ Gorgie Road ☎ 0131 623 7031 🚌 2, 3, 4, 12

Laserquest

Arcade and computer games systems are available, as well as the ultimate laser game for older children, stalking an opponent through a smoke-filled battle zone.
✉ 28 Bread Street ☎ 0131 221 0000 ⏰ Mon–Sat 11–11; Sun 11–10 🚌 1, 2, 6, 10, 12

Lauriston Castle

A fascinating look at Edwardian life in a 16th-century fortified house, with period furniture and furnishings, and large gardens to run around in (➤ 40).
✉ Cramond Road South, Davidson's Mains ☎ 0131 336 2060 ⏰ Apr–Oct Sat–Thu 11–1 and 2–5; Nov–Mar Sat, Sun 2–4. Guided tours only 🚌 40, 41, 80B

Leith Waterworld

A state-of-the-art leisure pool, particularly suitable for children, with a wide range of facilities, wave machine and water flume at the foot of Easter Road.

✉ 377 Easter Road ☎ 0131 555 6000 🕐 Wed–Thu 10–1; Fri–Sun 10–5 (open longer hours in school holidays)

Maid of the Forth

Enjoy a spectacular cruise from beneath the historic Forth Rail Bridge, with visits to the abbey on Inchcolm Island and close encounters with seals and dolphins (► 121). Evening cruises for grown-ups are also available (► 112).

✉ Hawes Pier, South Queensferry ☎ 0131 331 4857 (for sailing times) 🕐 Easter–Oct 🚌 43, 47

St Margaret's Loch

An ideal picnic spot when the weather is fine, just to feed the many swans and ducks, play football, fly kites and throw frisbees.

✉ Holyrood Park 🕐 Open all year 🚌 1, 6

Scottish Agricultural Museum

This fascinating collection of farm machinery, implements and artefacts of countryside crafts has audio-visual programmes and changing displays that will interest children and adults alike.

✉ Ingliston ☎ 0131 333 2674 🕐 Apr–Sep daily 10–5; Oct–Mar Mon–Fri 10–5 🚌 Airline 100

Tartan Weaving Mill and Exhibition

Children will enjoy following the stages in the production of wool from sheep to the finished article with working looms and kiltmakers; there is also an exhibition of Highland dress.

✉ 555 Castlehill ☎ 0131 226 1555 🕐 Daily 9–5:30 🚌 1, 6

Witchery Tour

Older children will be enthralled and not a little frightened by the Ghost and Gore, or Murder and Mystery, tours led by convincing guides through the darker parts of Old Edinburgh.

✉ 352 Castlehill, Royal Mile ☎ 0131 225 6745 🚌 1, 6, 34, 35

Outside Edinburgh

Livingston
Almond Valley Heritage Centre

Innovative museum of the history of West Lothian, with narrow-gauge railway, friendly farmyard animals, play areas and games and computers to provide an interesting day out for all the family.

✉ Millfield, Kirkton North ☎ 01506 414957 🕐 Mon–Sat 10–5 🚌 D27

East Lothian
Museum of Flight

There is a huge range of aeroplanes, rockets, models and aeronautica in two massive hangars on this World War II airfield east of Edinburgh, giving a great day out for all the family.

✉ East Fortune Airfield, near Haddington ☎ 01620 880308 🕐 Daily 10:30–5; Jul, Aug 10:30–6

North Queensferry
Deep-Sea World

Scotland's national aquarium at North Queensferry provides education and great entertainment in a purpose-designed environment. A special attraction is the world's longest underwater tunnel.

✉ North Queensferry ☎ 01383 411880 🕐 Mar–Oct daily 10–6; Nov–Feb Mon–Fri 11–5 (weekends, Bank Hols 10–6)

School Holidays

Scottish school holiday dates differ from English ones, so it makes sense to plan a trip with kids when Scots children are in school, and children's attractions are less crowded. Summer sees the main differences; Scottish schools break up at the end of June and go back mid-August, leaving a whole month (which covers the Festival dates) when Scottish children are back in the classroom and English ones still free.

Edinburgh

Edinburgh Buses

All the buses listed in this guide are operated by Lothian Regional Transport (LRT); they are coloured maroon and white and operate all over the city. You'll also see buses run by other companies on the streets, many of them using duplicate routes. It's strongly recommended that you pick up a bus guide and travel map. LRT offer both travel and tourist passes and also operate a 24-hour help and information line (☎ 0131 555 6363). (► 21).

Lothian Regional Transport Travelshop

✉ 27 Hanover Street
☎ 0131 554 4494

Cinemas

ABC Multiplex

A modern cinema complex to the west of the city, with eight screens showing the full range of up-to-date commercial movies in great comfort.

✉ **Westside Plaza, 120 Wester Hailes Road** ☎ **0131 453 3332** 🚌 **3, 28, 30**

Cameo

A small but comfortable independent West End cinema which specialises in new art-house releases and cult late-night movies.

✉ **38 Home Street** ☎ **0131 228 4141** 🚌 **10, 11, 15, 16**

Dominion Cinema

This old-fashioned cinema has a friendly atmosphere, and shows the latest releases in comfort and style. Situated on the south side of the city.

✉ **18 Newbattle Terrace** ☎ **0131 447 4771** 🚌 **5, 11, 15, 16**

Filmhouse

A public independent cinema, showing an eclectic range of art-house and classic movies, with top-quality films from around the world.

✉ **88 Lothian Road** ☎ **0131 228 2688** 🚌 **1, 2, 6, 10, 12**

The Lumière

This modern cinema is attached to the new Museum of Scotland building (► 19). The programme consists of a limited week-end selection of classic, mainstream and art-house movies.

✉ **Chambers Street** ☎ **0131 247 4219** 🚌 **2, 3, 5, 12, 23**

MGM's ABC

This cinema offers the best of big-screen entertainment in the West End of the city, with dolby stereo in all three cinemas.

✉ **120 Lothian Road** ☎ **0131 228 1638** 🚌 **1, 2, 6, 10, 12**

Odeon Cinema

Centrally located cinema with five screens, showing the big commercial movies in pleasant surroundings with the latest sound systems.

✉ **7 Clerk Street** ☎ **0131 667 0971** 🚌 **2, 3, 5, 7**

UCI

Modern multiplex in retail park on the eastern outskirts of the city, showing a variety of mainstream movies with highest-quality sound reproduction on 12 screens.

✉ **7 Kinnaird Park, Newcraighall Road** ☎ **0131 669 0777** 🚌 **14, 14B, 32, 52**

Cultural Venues

Assembly Rooms

Popular venue for mainstream Festival Fringe productions, with an impressive ballroom and music hall. Ceilidhs, dances and gigs are held throughout the year (► 33).

✉ **54 George Street** ☎ **0131 220 4348** 🚌 **19, 20, 23, 27**

Church Hill Theatre

Municipally owned theatre that has professional companies during the Festival, and amateur productions of variable standards during the rest of the year.

✉ **33a Morningside Road** ☎ **0131 447 7597** 🚌 **5, 11, 15, 16**

Edinburgh Festival Theatre

Completed in 1994, this international theatre offers ballet, drama, variety and dance, as well as providing a base for all of Scottish Opera's Edinburgh performances, on one of the largest stages in Europe.

✉ **13–29 Nicolson Street**
☎ **0131 529 6000** 🚌 **2, 3, 5, 12**

Kings Theatre

A handsome Edwardian theatre, owned by the city, that presents a comprehensive range of drama, musicals, dance and pantomime, as well as international opera during the Festival.

✉ **2 Leven Street** ☎ **0131 529 6000** 🚌 **10, 11, 15, 16**

Playhouse Theatre

The multi-purpose auditorium can stage West End musicals, concerts of all sizes and leading rock groups. It also offers a range of corporate facilities and a cinema.

✉ **18–22 Greenside Place**
☎ **0131 557 2590** 🚌 **2, 10, 11, 12**

Queens Hall

This converted church hosts a wide variety of concerts, with contemporary and classical chamber music, as well as jazz, folk and rock music.

✉ **89 Clerk Street** ☎ **0131 668 2019** 🚌 **2, 3, 5, 12**

Ross Open Air Theatre

An open-air seasonal venue situated in Princes Street Gardens, staging a variety of performances throughout the summer, including children's shows, music and dance.

✉ **Princes Street Gardens**
☎ **0131 220 4351** 🚌 **3, 11, 21, 44**

Royal Lyceum Theatre Company

This magnificent Victorian theatre presents an integrated mix of classics and adaptations, with drama, tragedy, thrillers and comedy, as well as new works.

✉ **Grindlay Street** ☎ **0131 248 4848** 🚌 **1, 2, 6, 10, 12**

Traverse Theatre

Saltire Court is a state-of-the-art building completed in 1991. It provides a home for the leading theatre company in Scotland who stage original new productions.

✉ **Cambridge Street** ☎ **0131 228 1404** 🚌 **1, 2, 10, 12**

Usher Hall

The city's leading large-scale concert hall, built in 1913, is the base for the Scottish National Orchestra during the winter. The ideal venue for popular music concerts, and also available to hire for conferences.

✉ **Lothian Road** ☎ **0131 228 8616** 🚌 **1, 2, 6, 10, 12**

Motor Tours

Rabbie's Trail Burners

A wide choice of daily tours in a comfortable 16-seater minicoach are on offer; destinations include some of Scotland's most beautiful areas, including Loch Ness, Loch Lomond, Glencoe, The Trossachs and St Andrews. The tour coach drivers are knowledgeable and friendly.

✉ **207 High Street, Royal Mile**
☎ **0131 226 3133** 🚌 **1, 6, 34, 35**

City Bus Tours

If time is short you'll get a real taste of Edinburgh by using one of the guided tour services that wend their way from Waverley Station round the main sights. All operate a 'jump on and off' policy, so the ticket price allows you to pause to visit something, then join a later bus. Some have a lively commentary from a knowledgeable local guide, others favour the headphone approach (usually in several languages).

Guide Friday

✉ **133–5 Canongate, Royal Mile** ☎ **0131 556 2244**

Edinburgh Classic Tour

✉ **27 Hanover Street** ☎ **0131 554 4494**

Clubbing and Nightlife

It's always hard in any city to be aware of what's new on the club scene, and Edinburgh is no exception, with clubs coming and going and waxing and waning in popularity. Weekend nightlife centres around the venues in the West End, the Grassmarket and the Cowgate, all packed on Fridays and Saturdays. To find out what's on, buy *The List*, published weekly.

Nightclubs, Pubs and Scottish Entertainment

Bannerman's

This popular pub, in a series of huge rooms off Cowgate, has a great atmosphere, and is an ideal venue in which to amuse or be amused with video screens, dominoes, cribbage, cards, board games and substantial food.
✉ 212 Cowgate ☎ 0131 556 3254 🚌 2, 12

Bennet's Bar

An elaborate Victorian bar with authentic décor close to King's Theatre, ideal for drama fans and a perfect place to enjoy sound food and a pleasant ambience; closed Sunday lunch.
✉ 8 Leven Street ☎ 0131 229 5143 🚌 10, 11, 15, 16

Dalhousie Jacobean Banquet

A unique experience, set in 1623, with wine and mead served by comtemporarily dressed court ladies, and a banquet served to the haunting skirl of the pipes..
✉ Dalhousie Court Hotel, Cockpen Road, Bonnyrigg ☎ 0131 660 3200 🚌 Courtesy coach service (free)

Ensign Ewart

Close to Edinburgh Castle, this popular pub, named after a hero of Waterloo, offers good food and beer, and is noted for its regular folk music sessions.
✉ 521 Lawnmarket ☎ 0131 225 7440 🚌 1, 6, 23, 27

George Scottish Evening

Traditional entertainment in the opulent surroundings of the George Inter-Continental Hotel. Impressive five-course meal and resident host.
✉ 19–21 George Street ☎ 0131 225 1251 🚌 12, 22, 33, 51

Hail Caledonia Scottish Evening

An entertaining evening is offered in the Carlton Highland Hotel, with a range of typical Scottish fare and warm hospitality.
✉ Carlton Highland Hotel, North Bridge ☎ 0131 472 3000 🚌 3, 5, 7, 9

Jamie's Scottish Evening

For over 25 years this original Scottish show has entertained and delighted in the King James Thistle Hotel, with tasty dinner served before a programme of dancing, singing and bagpipes.
✉ 107 Leith Street ☎ 0131 556 0111 🚌 2, 7, 8, 9

Maid of the Forth

For something a little different, take a 3-hour evening cruise on the Firth of Forth, with licensed bar and live jazz or folk music, optional barbecue food and spectacular views of seals and the bridges (► 109 for daytime cruises.)
✉ Hawes Pier, South Queensferry ☎ 0131 331 4857 🚌 43, 47

Sheeps Heid Inn

One of the oldest coaching inns in Scotland, this old-fashioned Duddingston hostelry retains a congenial atmosphere, with beer and skittles, ideal for a pleasant summer visit.
✉ 43 The Causeway, Duddingston ☎ 0131 656 6951 🚌 4, 42, 45

The Subway

One of Edinburgh's busiest clubs is to be found in darkest Cowgate, featuring live music from emerging bands alternating with a wide range of contemporary pop.

✉ **69 Cowgate** ☎ **0131 225 6766** 🚌 **2, 12**

A Taste of Scotland

An extravaganza of traditional Scottish entertainment and cuisine held in the magnificent historic setting of the converted stables of Prestonfield House Hotel during the summer.

✉ **Prestonfield House Hotel, Priestfield Road** ☎ **0131 668 3346** 🚌 **2, 12, 14, 21**

The Vaults

Very popular nightclub in the vaults supporting South Bridge, a maze of dance floors and bars, with hard house and techno dance music on Wed to Sat nights.

✉ **15–17 Niddry Street** ☎ **0131 558 9052** 🚌 **2, 12**

Whigham Wine Cellars

This series of candle-lit basement vaults off Charlotte Square supplies the perfect environment for chilling out to relaxing music, with good food and wines.

✉ **13 Hope Street** ☎ **0131 225 9717** 🚌 **19, 34, 35**

Whistle Binkie's

Open from early evening until the small hours, this cosy pub is centrally located and provides live music seven nights a week – an excellent place to enjoy a sociable drink.

✉ **6 Niddry Street** ☎ **0131 557 5114** 🚌 **2, 12**

Sport

Angling

Glencorse Reservoir

Attractive upland loch in pleasant scenic surroundings south of Edinburgh, with hatchery-maintained stock of brown and rainbow trout offering excellent boat fishing Apr–Sep.

✉ **Glencorse Reservoir** ☎ **0131 445 6462**

Association Football

Easter Road

East of the city centre: the ground of the Hibernian Football Club, or Hibs, which plays professional football here during the season, August to May, chiefly on every other Saturday.

✉ **Easter Road Stadium, Albion Place** ☎ **0131 661 2159** 🚌 **1, 6, 13, 24 (A)**

Tynecastle

To the west of the city, and home of the Heart of Midlothian Football Club, or Hearts. Professional football is played here mostly on alternate Saturday afternoons between August and May.

✉ **Tynecastle Park, Gorgie Road** ☎ **0131 337 6132** 🚌 **1, 2, 3, 6, 12**

Athletics

Meadowbank Sports Centre and Stadium

This is the city's main venue for athletic meetings. As well as a velodrome, it also offers facilities for squash, basketball and badminton in a series of indoor halls.

✉ **139 London Road** ☎ **0131 661 5351** 🚌 **15, 26, 45**

The Gay Scene

Edinburgh has a thriving, friendly and reasonably open gay scene. There are hotels, clubs, cafés and pubs that cater exclusively for the gay community, and safety levels are high, with a police liaison officer who helps deal with any problems. The scene centres around Broughton Street, an area known as the Pink Triangle, which should be your first port of call to check out what's happening.

Massage Parlours

Don't be tempted to head for a city-centre massage parlour or sauna, unless you're looking for other services. In a highly successful drive to move prostitution off the streets, the city council has long licensed these establishments under the health and safety regulations, making them definitely not-the-place for families to relax after a day's sightseeing.

Sport

Angling

Glencorse Reservoir

Attractive upland loch in pleasant scenic surroundings south of Edinburgh, with hatchery-maintained stock of brown and rainbow trout offering excellent boat fishing Apr–Sep.

✉ **Glencorse Reservoir**
☎ **0131 445 6462**

Association Football

Easter Road

East of the city centre: the ground of the Hibernian Football Club, or Hibs, which plays professional football here during the season, August to May, chiefly on every other Saturday.

✉ **Easter Road Stadium, Albion Place** ☎ **0131 661 2159** 🚌 **1, 6, 13, 24 (A)**

Tynecastle

To the west of the city, and home of the Heart of Midlothian Football Club, or Hearts. Professional football is played here mostly on alternate Saturday afternoons between August and May.

✉ **Tynecastle Park, Gorgie Road** ☎ **0131 337 6132** 🚌 **1, 2, 3, 6, 12**

Athletics

Meadowbank Sports Centre and Stadium

This is the city's main venue for athletic meetings. As well as a velodrome, it also offers facilities for squash, basketball and badminton in a series of indoor halls.

✉ **139 London Road** ☎ **0131 661 5351** 🚌 **15, 26, 45**

Cricket

Grange Cricket Club

This pleasant Stockbridge ground was the venue for two matches during the 1999 World Cup, and hosts a number of games in the summer, chiefly on Saturdays.

✉ **Raeburn Place, Musselburgh** ☎ **0131 3177247** 🚌 **19, 20, 28**

Golf

Braid Hills Golf Course

Golfers enjoy the bonus of superb views of Edinburgh and the Firth of Forth from this challenging and hilly municipally owned course to the south of the city. The course boasts some excellent holes.

✉ **Braid Hills Approach** ☎ **0131 447 6666** 🚌 **11, 15(A)**

Craigmillar Park Golf Course

Close to the Royal Scottish Observatory (► 61), this private course welcomes visitors to play over its sloping holes. The course is located near Blackford Hill, with fine views over Edinburgh.

✉ **1 Observatory Road** ☎ **0131 667 0047** 🚌 **2, 12, 14, 21**

Silverknowes Golf Course

This municipally owned course is pleasantly situated close to the Firth of Forth, and the gently undulating terrain presents some challenging holes for local golfers and visitors.

✉ **Silverknowes Parkway** ☎ **0131 336 3843** 🚌 **8, 9, 14, 27**

Horse-racing

Musselburgh Racecourse

Ten kilometres (6 miles) east of Edinburgh is this pleasant racecourse beside the Firth of Forth, one of the oldest in the country. There are over 20 meetings throughout the year here.

✉ **Linkfield Road** ☎ **0131 665 2859** 🚌 **15, 26, 43**

Ice Skating

Murrayfield Ice Rink

The Murrayfield rink, next to the rugby stadium, is home also the home base for the Edinburgh ice hockey team. There are sessions for beginners and more accomplished skaters.

✉ **Riversdale Crescent** ☎ **0131 337 6933** 🚌 **2, 12, 26**

Rugby Union Football

Murrayfield Stadium

This impressive stadium to the west of the city centre is home to the Scottish national team, and the venue for most of the international matches are played on occasional Saturdays.

✉ **Murrayfield Stadium, Corstorphine Road,** ☎ **0131 346 5000** 🚌 **2, 12, 26**

Sailing

Port Edgar Sailing School

The largest watersport centre in Scotland, on the Firth of Forth, close to the bridges, with tuition and boat hire for dinghy and catamaran sailing, canoeing and powerboating.

✉ **Shore Road, South Queensferry** ☎ **0131 331 3330** 🚌 **43, 47**

Skiing

Midlothian Ski Centre

Europe's longest artificial ski slope, with chairlift facilities for skiers and sightseers.

✉ **Hillend** ☎ **0131 445 4433** 🚌 **4**

Swimming

Glenogle

Attractive Victorian swimming pool, with lots of cast iron and cosy atmosphere, sauna and fitness centre, close to New Town.

✉ **Glenogle Road** ☎ **0131 343 6376** 🚌 **20, 28, 80**

Royal Commonwealth Pool

Olympic-sized swimming pool, with diving pools, fitness centre and sauna, water flumes and beginners' area in impressive building constructed for the 1970 Commonwealth Games.

✉ **Dalkeith Road** ☎ **0131 667 7211** 🚌 **2, 12, 14, 21**

Tennis

Craiglockhart Tennis and Sports Centre

There are six indoor and eight outdoor courts in this southside sports centre, as well as badminton and squash courts, and a fitness centre.

✉ **177 Colinton Road** ☎ **0131 444 1969 (tennis centre); 0131 443 0101 (sports centre)** 🚌 **10, 27, 45, 47**

Guided Tours

Caledonian Brewery Visitor Centre

A chance to discover the secrets of producing top-quality ale, brewed with original equipment, from steeping to fermentation, in

Care in the Countryside

If you're spending a few days exploring Edinburgh's environs, you may be tempted to take to the hills for a day's strenuous exercise. If you do, make sure you are properly equipped, with good boots, wind- and waterproofs and something to eat and drink. Take a map and let someone know where you're heading and what time you expect to be back. The Scottish hills can be dangerous, with quick weather changes.

What's On When

Festival Booking
Many festival-goers do not book.

Edinburgh International Festival
✉ The Hub, Castlehill, Royal Mile, Edinburgh EH1 2NE
☎ 0131 473 2000/2001

Websites:
information info@eif.co.uk
tickets boxoffice@eif.co.uk

The Fringe
✉ The Fringe Office, 180 High Street, Royal Mile, Ediburgh EH1
☎ 0131 226 5257;

Website:
www.edfringe.com

Edinburgh Military Tattoo
✉ Castle Esplanade, Edinburgh Castle
☎ 0131 225 1188

Edinburgh Film Festival
✉ Filmhouse, 88 Lothian Road, Edinburgh
☎ 0131 229 2550/ 228 4051

Edinburgh Book Festival
✉ Charlotte Square, Edinburgh EH2 ☎ 0131 228 5444/5424

January
Edinburgh Hogmanay
This spectacular 3-day street party, centred on Princes Street, has become Europe's biggest winter festival, with street theatre, ceilidhs and general merrymaking.

Burns Night
Edinburgh celebrates the birthday of Scotland's national poet on January 25, with traditional haggis dinners and draughts of whisky in hotels and restaurants all over the city.

April
Edinburgh Science Festival
Lectures and events covering all branches of science and technology, held in over 40 venues city-wide.

May
Museum Week
Annual event to raise the profile of Edinburgh museums, with a series of art workshops, guided walks and exhibitions.

Scottish International Children's Festival
The largest festival of performing arts in the UK for children and young people.

June
Royal Highland Show
Highlight of Scotland's country year, with huge variety of events, including pedigree livestock judging, show-jumping and agricultural displays, over five days.

August
Edinburgh International Festival
Three weeks of top-quality opera, dance, music and theatre from all around the

world, at a variety of locations throughout the city.

Edinburgh Festival Fringe
The world's largest arts festival, held over three weeks, including exhibitions, music, dance, comedy and shows for children.

Edinburgh Military Tattoo
A spectacular display of music, entertainment and theatre with a military theme, set against the stunning backdrop of Edinburgh Castle.

Edinburgh International Film Festival
The world's longest-running film festival has both main-stream and independent new releases, with interviews, discussions and debate.

Book Festival
An annual event since 1998, the festival occupies a tented village in Charlotte Square, and attracts a wide spectrum of authors.

Jazz and Blues Festival
The complete gamut of jazz forms can be found in the many venues that host this international festival.

September
Firework Concert
A fantastic firework display against the backdrop of the Castle, accompanied by classical music.

Open Doors Day
Some of the finest private houses in Edinburgh are opened to members of the public on one day of the year; contact the Cockburn Association, Trunk's Close, 55 High Street EH1 1SR (☎ 0131 557 8686).

Practical Matters

Above: *the Traverse Theatre's brightly
coloured neon sign*
Below: *signposts to some of Edinburgh's
many attractions*

TIME DIFFERENCES

→
GMT
12 noon

Edinburgh
12 noon

→
Germany
1PM

←
USA (NY)
7AM

→
Netherlands
1PM

→
Spain
1PM

BEFORE YOU GO

WHAT YOU NEED

	UK	Germany	USA	Netherlands	Spain
● Required					
○ Suggested					
▲ Not required					
Passport	▲	●	●	●	●
Visa	▲	▲	▲	▲	▲
Onward or Return Ticket	▲	▲	●	▲	▲
Health Inoculations	▲	▲	▲	▲	▲
Health Documentation (➤ 123, Health)	▲	▲	▲	▲	▲
Travel Insurance	○	○	○	○	○
Driving Licence (national or International)	●	●	●	●	●
Car Insurance Certificate (if own car)	●	●	●	●	●
Car Registration Document (if own car)	●	●	●	●	●

WHEN TO GO

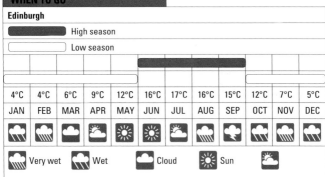

Edinburgh

High season

Low season

4°C	4°C	6°C	9°C	12°C	16°C	17°C	16°C	15°C	12°C	7°C	5°C
JAN	FEB	MAR	APR	MAY	JUN	JUL	AUG	SEP	OCT	NOV	DEC

Very wet   Wet   Cloud   Sun

TOURIST OFFICES

In the UK
Edinburgh and Lothians
Tourist Board
4 Rothesay Terrace
Edinburgh EH3 7RY
☎ 0131 473 3800
fax 0131 473 3881
website
www.edinburgh.org

Scottish Tourist Board
23 Ravelston Terrace
Edinburgh EH4 3TP
☎ 0131 332 2433
fax 0131 343 1513
website
www.holiday.scotland.net

In the USA
British Tourist Authority
551 Fifth Avenue, Suite 701
New York
NY 10176–0799
☎ 001 212 986 2266

POLICE	999
FIRE	999
AMBULANCE	999
RED CROSS	0131 557 9898

WHEN YOU ARE THERE

ARRIVING

Britain's national airline, British Airways (☎ 0345 222 111), has frequent scheduled flights in and out of Edinburgh; the airport is also served by British Midland, Air France, Aer Lingus, KLM, Lufthansa, Sabena and Easyjet. Passengers arriving in Britain on intercontinental flights will normally have to route via London.

Edinburgh Airport
to city centre

16 kilometres (10 miles)

Journey times

 N/A

🚌 30 minutes

🚗 15–20 minutes

MONEY

Scotland's currency is pounds sterling (£) issued by the three major Scottish banks (the Bank of Scotland, the Royal Bank of Scotland and the Clydesdale Bank) in notes of £1, £5, £10, £20, £50 and £100. Bank of England notes are legal tender and all coins are issued by the Royal Mint; there are 1p, 2p, 5p, 10p, 20p, £1 and £2 coins. You can exchange foreign currency and travellers' cheques at banks and bureaux de change; banks are generally open 9AM–4PM. Cashpoint machines can be found outside banks and building societies and operate 24 hours a day; they accept bank cards and also allow you advances on many credit cards.

TIME

 Like those in the rest of the UK, Scottish clocks go forward by one hour on the last weekend in March to give British Summer Time (BST). Clocks go back to rejoin Greenwich Mean Time (GMT) the last weekend in October.

CUSTOMS

 YES
Goods Bought Outside the EU (Limits):
Alcohol (over 22° vol): 1L or
Alcohol (not over 22° vol): 2L
and Still table wine: 2L
Cigarettes: 200 or Cigars: 50 or
Tobacco: 250gms
Perfume: 60ml
Toilet water: 250ml
Goods Bought Duty and Tax Paid Inside the EU (Guidance Levels):
Alcohol (over 22° vol): 10L and
Alcohol (not over 22° vol): 20L
and wine (max 60L sparkling):
90L and beer: 110L
Cigarettes: 800 and
Cigars: 200 and
Tobacco: 1kg
Perfume: no limit
Toilet water: no limit
Visitors under 17 are not entitled to the alcohol and tobacco allowances.

NO
Drugs, offensive weapons, obscene material, unlicensed animals. Sportsmen may bring sporting firearms and the necessary ammunition into the UK on the production of the relevant documentation.

CONSULTATES

USA:
09068 200290

Germany
0131 337 2323
fax 0131 346 1578

Netherlands
0131 220 3226

Spain
0131 220 1843
fax 0131 226 4568

WHEN YOU ARE THERE

TOURIST OFFICES

Edinburgh and Scotland Information Centre
● Princes Mall
  3 Princes Street
  EH12 2QP
  ☎ 0131 473 3800
  Fax 0131 473 3881

Edinburgh Airport Tourist Information Desk
● Ingliston
  EH12 9DN
  ☎ 0131 333 2167
  Fax 0131 335 3576

St Andrews
● 70 Market Street
  Fife KY16 9NU
  ☎ 01334 472021
  Fax 01334 478422

Linlithgow
● Burgh Halls
  The Cross
  EH49 7AH
  ☎ 01506 844600
  Fax 01506 671373

Glasgow
● 11 George Sq
  G2 1DY
  ☎ 0141 204 4400
  Fax 0141 221 3524

North Berwick
● Quality Street
  EH39 4HJ
  ☎ 01620 892197
  Fax 01620 893667

Peebles
● High Street
  EH45 8AG
  ☎ 01721 720138
  Fax 01721 724401

Stirling
● 41 Dumbarton Road
  FK8 2LQ
  ☎ 01786 475019

NATIONAL HOLIDAYS

J	F	M	A	M	J	J	A	S	O	N	D
2		(1)	(1)	2		1	1	1			2

Scottish public holidays may vary from place to place and their dates from year to year; thus, although Edinburgh may be on holiday at certain times, other Scottish towns and cities will not necessarily be having a public holiday. Major holidays are:

1 Jan	*New Year's Day
2 Jan	*Holiday
Mar/Apr	*Good Friday, Easter Monday
First Mon May	*May Day Bank Holiday
Mon, mid–late May	Victoria Holiday
From 1st Mon in July	Edinburgh Trades Holiday 2 wks
Last Mon in Aug	August Bank Holiday
3rd Mon in Sep	Autumn Holiday
25 Dec	*Christmas Day
26 Dec	*Boxing Day
	* throughout Scotland

OPENING HOURS

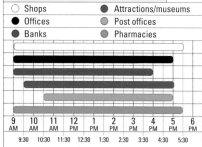

In addition, most shops in central Edinburgh are open until 8PM on Thu and many open 12–5 on Sun. Tourist-oriented shops are also open on Sun all over the city, as is the Gyle Centre, a huge out-of-town shopping centre on the western outskirts. Some city-centre banks remain open until 5 or 5:30. Edinburgh has all-day licensing in its pubs and bars, which are normally open 11AM–11PM or later.

DRIVE ON THE
LEFT

TOILETS
FREE

PUBLIC TRANSPORT

Internal Flights to Aberdeen, Inverness, Kirkwall, Sumburgh, and Wick; also to Birmingham, Bournemouth, Bristol, East Midlands, Guernsey, Humberside, Jersey, London Heathrow, London Gatwick, London Stansted, Manchester, Norwich and Southampton in England. For the Western Isles, fly from Glasgow Airport.

Trains Edinburgh has two mainline railway stations: Edinburgh Waverley and Edinburgh Haymarket. Most internal rail services are run by Scotrail. You can get details of fares and services by calling the National Rail Enquiry Scheme (☎ 0345 484950) or by calling in person at the information desk in Waverley Station.

Buses Coaches arrive in Edinburgh from England, Wales and all over Scotland at the St Andrew Square Bus Station; National Express (☎ 0990 80 80 80) serving English destinations and Scottish Citylink (☎ 0990 50 50 50) Scottish. Other Scottish bus companies also operate into the terminal, where there is an information office.

Boat Trips The *Maid of the Forth* leaves daily from Hawes Pier, South Queensferry, sailing beneath the Forth Rail Bridge to Inchcolm Island between Easter and October (☎ 0131 331 4857). From North Berwick, the *Sula* sails 2 to 4 times daily to the Bass Rock between Easter and September (☎ 01620 892838).

Urban Transport Pay on boarding, making sure you have the correct fare. The chief Edinburgh operator is Lothian Regional Transport (LRT). For general information ☎ 0131 0800 23 23 23 (local calls), 0131 225 3858 (national calls); LRT have two travel shops (27 Hanover Street and Waverley Bridge, Princes Street).

CAR RENTAL

Local firms include Arnold Clark (☎ 0131 228 4747), Alexander's Car Rental (☎ 0131 229 3331) and Practical Car and Van Rental (☎ 0131 661 2222). Major rental firms such as Avis, Hertz and Budget have offices at Edinburgh Airport (☎ 0131 333 1000).

TAXIS

Edinburgh Airport Taxis (☎ 0131 344 3344/3153) are white; city centre taxis are black and can be hailed on the street, picked up at ranks or you can call Capital Castle Taxis (☎ 0131 228 2555), City Cabs (☎ 0131 228 1211) or Edinburgh Taxis (☎ 0131 228 8989).

DRIVING

Speed limit on motorways: **110kph (70mph)**

Speed limit on main roads: **100kph (60mph)**

Speed limit on minor roads: **50–65kph (30–40mph)** advisable and compulsory in built-up areas.

Must be worn in front and back seats at all times

Random Breath Testing. Limit: 30ml on breath/80ml in blood.

Non-leaded, leaded and diesel fuel is available from all service stations. This normally comes in three grades, premium unleaded, 4-star and city diesel. Petrol stations are normally open 6AM–10PM Mon–Sat and 8AM–8PM on Sundays, though some (often self-service) are open 24 hours. All take credit and direct debit cards and many have well-stocked shops.

If you break down driving your own car you can call the AA and join on the spot if you are not already a member (☎ 0800 887766). If you are driving a hire car, call the emergency number given you by the hire company in the documentation; most rental firms provide a rescue service.

121

Ruler markings:

CENTIMETRES 0 1 2 3 4 5 6 7 8

INCHES 0 1 2 3

PERSONAL SAFETY

Scots policemen wear a peaked flat hat with a black-and-white chequered band; they are friendly and approachable and will give directions and information willingly. On the whole, tourist Edinburgh is exceptionally safe and you should have no problems if you take sensible precautions:

- Do not carry more cash than you need
- Beware of pickpockets, particularly in the main tourist areas

Police assistance:
☎ **999**
from any call box

- Areas to avoid at night include: backstreet and dockside areas of Leith, wynds leading off Royal Mile, the footpaths across the Meadows and some peripheral housing schemes. Only call 999 for true emergencies.

ELECTRICITY

The power supply in Edinburgh is: 240 volts AC.

Sockets accept three-pin plugs. North American visitors will need a transformer and adaptor for electrical appliances, European and Australasian visitors an adaptor only.

TELEPHONES

Public telephone boxes are operated by BT and other telephone companies. Calls can be made using credit cards, phone company credit cards, phone cards (available in units of £2, £5 and £10) and coins. The Edinburgh code is 0131; dial 100 to call the operator, and 192 for directory enquiries.

International Dialling Codes

From Edinburgh to:
UK: n/a
Germany: 00 49
USA and Canada: 00 1
Netherlands: 00 31

POST

Post offices are open 9AM–5:30PM Mon–Fri and 9AM–12:30PM on Sat; Edinburgh's main post office at the St James Centre is also open until 6PM on Sat. For Royal Mail queries contact Customer Services (☎ 0345 740740). You can buy stamps in many gift shops, general stores and supermarkets as well as in post offices.

TIPS/GRATUITIES

Yes ✓	No ✗	
Restaurants (service not included)	✓	10–15%
Cafés/bars (change if table service)	✓	
Tour guides	✓	10%
Taxis	✓	10%
Porters (depending amount of luggage)	✓	£1–3
Chambermaids	✓	change
Theatre/cinema Usherettes	✗	
Hairdressers	✓	10%
Cloakroom attendants	✓	5p–10p
Toilets	✓	5p–10p

PHOTOGRAPHY

What to photograph: Views of the city from the castle, Calton Hill and Arthur's Seat; the city skyline; buildings in the Royal Mile and New Town, parks and gardens, picturesque corners and squares.

When to photograph: Light levels in the north allow photography all day; check your light metre before photographing. Sunsets can be spectacular.

Where to buy film: Chemists, specialist photography shops, tourist and gift shops.

HEALTH

Doctors
The National Health Service (NHS) provides free treatment for all EU nationals and residents of countries with which the UK has a reciprocal agreement. Accident and emergency treatment is free to everyone. The 24-hour casualty department is at the Royal Infirmary of Edinburgh, 1 Lauriston Place (☎ 0131 536 4000).

Dental Services
Dental services are free only to UK citizens who fall into certain categories. For emergencies, there are two free walk-in dental clinics in Edinburgh: the Edinburgh Dental Institute, Level 7, Lauriston Building, 1 Lauriston Place (☎ 0131 536 4913) and the Western General Hospital, Crewe Road South (☎ 0131 537 1338).

Sun Advice
You are unlikely to get sunburnt in Edinburgh as there are few completely sunny days. However, sunshine is often accompanied by a good breeze and you may be unaware of the UV radiation levels of the sun in these northern latitudes; so you should still take care.

Drugs
Prescription and non-prescription drugs and medicine are available from chemists, often distinguished by a green cross. Some supermarkets also have a chemist's shop within the store. Chemists can advise on treatment for simple complaints.

Safe Water
Tap water in Edinburgh is safe and reasonably palatable; bottled water is widely available in bars, restaurants and food stores.

CONCESSIONS

Students will get reduced-cost entry into museums, galleries and some attractions on the production of a valid student card. As a university city, Edinburgh is well provided with good-value bars, clubs and restaurants, while its role as Scotland's capital means that a wide range of budget accommodation and hostels is on offer.

Senior citizens are eligible for reduced-cost entry into museums, galleries and some attractions on the production of identification. Bus and train fares for excursions outside Edinburgh will be cheaper for those showing a valid bus or train senior citizen's card.

CLOTHING SIZES

USA	UK	Europe	
36	36	46	
38	38	48	
40	40	50	
42	42	52	Suits
44	44	54	
46	46	56	
8	7	41	
8.5	7.5	42	
9.5	8.5	43	
10.5	9.5	44	Shoes
11.5	10.5	45	
12	11	46	
14.5	14.5	37	
15	15	38	
15.5	15.5	39/40	
16	16	41	Shirts
16.5	16.5	42	
17	17	43	
6	8	34	
8	10	36	
10	12	38	
12	14	40	Dresses
14	16	42	
16	18	44	
6	4.5	38	
6.5	5	39	
7	5.5	39	
7.5	6	39	Shoes
8	6.5	40	
8.5	7	41	

WHEN DEPARTING

- If you are leaving Ediburgh by air, British Airways flights do not need re-confirming.
- If you have been in Edinburgh on a package holiday, contact your holiday operator or their representative to confirm your departure details.
- You should have no problem with customs officials.

LANGUAGE

You'll have no difficulty in understanding the people of Edinburgh, who tend automatically to modulate their accent when speaking to non-Scots. But there are many words and expressions that are uniquely Scots and used in everyday conversation, here are a few:

auld	old; Edinburgh is often called Auld Reekie, a reference to its smoking chimney-pots which once cast a pall over the city
awfy	very; a person might be described as 'awfy auld'
belong	come from; an Edinburgh native says 'I belong tae Edinburgh'
ben	mountain; Ben Nevis is the highest in Scotland and the UK
blether	to chatter or a garrulous person; 'she's an awfy blether'
bonnie	pretty, attractive; 'that's a bonnie blink' meaning a fine view
brae	slope or hillside
braw	fine, 'he's a braw laddie'
burn	stream
cairn	a pile of stones, often on the top of a hill or acting as a memorial
ceilidh	an informal gathering to tell stories and singsongs; now often an organised entertainment with a Scottish theme
clan	Highland tribe or family group owing allegiance to a chief
couthy	homely and comfortable
douce	gentle and kind; can be used to describe weather conditions
dram	a drink of whisky
dreich	dreary, wet and dull; used about the weather but also about people and gatherings
first-foot	the first visit paid to neighbours and friends after the start of New Year, traditionally with a bottle of whisky
fouter	fiddle around
glen	a Highland valley
gloaming	dusk
guttered	drunk
haar	fine summer sea mist found on east coast
harling	mixture of limestone and gravel used to cover exterior house walls
hen	affectionate and informal mode of address to a female
Hogmanay	New Year's Eve
ken	to know; either a fact or a person 'D'ye ken the High Street?', 'I dinnae ken Jock Fisher'
kirk	church
laird	estate landowner
lassie	girl
lugs	ears
lum	chimney; as in 'lang may your lum reek' – ie good health
manse	vicarage; the home of the minister
messages	food shopping; 'I'm awa' tae get the messages'
policies	grounds or parkland surrounding a substantial house
pend	vaulted passage or archway
quaich	a two-handled drinking bowl
sarnie	sandwich
Sassenach	originally a non-Gaelic speaking Lowlander, now usually a non-Scot
scunnered	displeased, fed up
stay	live; 'I stay in Edinburgh'
stravaig	wander aimlessly, and pleasurably, about
stushie	argument, fight
trews	tartan trousers
wynd	narrow lane between houses

Acknowledgements
The Automobile Association wishes to thank the following photographers and libraries for their assistance in the preparation of this book.

DYNAMIC EARTH 17b, 17c; MARY EVANS PICTURE LIBRARY 10b, 14; ILLUSTRATED LONDON NEWS 14c; KEN PATERSON 1, 8b, 8c, 42b, 42c, 53b; REX FEATURES 14; SPECTRUM COLOUR LIBRARY Front Cover (c) Piper.

The remaining photographs are held in the Association's own library (AA PHOTO LIBRARY) and were taken by Ken Paterson with the exception of the following: M Alexander 73, 74a, 75a, 76, 81a, 82a, 83a, 85a, 86a, 87a, 88a, 89a; Adrian Baker 43b, 43c, 90; Jim Carnie 82b, 82c, 87b; Douglas Corrance 5, 13c, 27b, 36b, 38b, 40a, 48c, 69b, 91a, 92, 93, 94, 95, 96, 97, 98, 99, 100, 101, 102, 103, 104, 105, 106, 107, 108, 109, 110, 111, 112, 113, 114, 115, 116; Steve Day 89b; Richard Elliot 5a, 6a, 7a, 8a, 9a, 10a, 11a, 12a, 13a, 14a, 20b, 30, 75b, 86c; Stephen Gibson 74b; Michael Taylor 84, 85b,

The photographer would like to thank the following for their assistance: HISTORIC SCOTLAND, NATIONAL TRUST FOR SCOTLAND, EDINBURGH CITY COUNCIL.

Editor: Jane Gregory   Copy editor: Susie Whimster   Page layout: Nautilus Design (UK) Ltd